TEACHING SECONDARY ENGLISH

General Editor: Peter King

TEACHING THE BASIC SKILLS

TEACHING THE BASIC SKILLS

Spelling, punctuation and grammar
in secondary English

DON SMEDLEY

London   METHUEN   *New York*

First published in 1983 by
Methuen & Co. Ltd
11 New Fetter Lane, London EC4P
4EE

Published in the USA by
Methuen & Co.
in association with Methuen, Inc.
733 Third Avenue, New York, NY
10017

© *1983 Don Smedley*

Phototypeset by Tradespools Ltd,
Frome, Somerset
Printed in Great Britain by
Richard Clay (The Chaucer Press)
Suffolk

British Library Cataloguing in
Publication Data
Smedley, Don
Teaching the basic skills.—(Teaching
secondary English)
1. English language—Grammar—
1950-
I. Title   II. Series
428   P1112

ISBN 0–416–34140–3
ISBN 0–416–34150–0 Pbk

CONTENTS

GENERAL EDITOR'S PREFACE

English remains a core subject in the secondary school curriculum as the confident words of a recent HMI document reveal:—

> English is of vital importance in the development of pupils as individuals and as members of society: our language is our principal means of making sense of our experience and communication with others. The teaching of English is concerned with the essential skills of speech, reading and writing, and with literature. Schools will doubtless continue to give them high priority.
>
> (*The School Curriculum*, DES, 1981)

Such confidence belies the fact that there has been, and continues to be, much debate among practitioners as to exactly what constitutes English. If the desired consensus remains rather far off at least the interested teacher now has a large and useful literature on which he or she can profitably reflect in the attempt to answer the question 'What is English?' There have been notable books designed to reorientate teachers' thinking about the subject ranging from those absorbed by the necessary theoretical analysis, like John Dixon's *Growth Through English* (Oxford, rev. edn 1975), to those working outwards from new research into classroom language, like *From Communication to Curriculum*, by Douglas Barnes (Penguin, 1976); but there are not so many books intended to help teachers get a purchase on their day-to-day activities (a fine exception is *The English Department Handbook* recently published by the ILEA English Centre). To gain such a purchase requires confidence built not from making 'everything new' so much as learning to combine the best from the older traditions with some of those newer ideas. And preferably these ideas have to be seen to have emerged from effective classroom teaching. The English teacher's aims have to be continually reworked in the light of new experience, and the assurance necessary to manage this is bred out of the convictions of other experienced practitioners. This is of particular importance to the new and inexperienced teacher. It is to such teachers and student teachers that this series is primarily directed.

The books in this series are intended to give practical guidance in the various areas of the English curriculum. Each area is treated in a separate volume in order to gain the necessary space in which to discuss it at some length. The aim of the series is twofold: to describe good practice by exploring the approaches and activities reflected in the daily work of an English teacher in the comprehensive school; and to give a practical lead to teachers who wish to try out for themselves a wider repertoire of teaching skills and ways of organizing syllabuses and lessons. Taken as a whole, the series does not press upon the reader a ready-made philosophy, but attempts to provide a map of the English teaching landscape in which the separate volumes highlight an individual feature of that terrain, representing its particular characteristics while re-minding us of the continuity between these differing elements in the overall topography.

The series addresses itself to the 11–16 age range with an additional volume on sixth-form work, and assumes a mixed ability grouping, at least in the first two years of schooling. Each volume begins with a discussion of the problems and rationale of its chosen aspect of English and goes on to describe practical ways in which the teachers can organize their syllabus and lessons to achieve their intended goals, and ends with a brief guide to books, resources, etc. The individual volumes are written by experienced teachers with a particular interest in their chosen area and the ideas they express have been proved by them or their colleagues in their own classrooms.

It is at the level of the practical that any synthesis of the various approaches to English can be gained, and to accomplish this every teacher must be in possession of a rationale and an awareness of good methods wherever and however they have been achieved. By reading the books in this series it is to be hoped that teachers will be encouraged to try out for themselves ideas found effective by their colleagues so gaining the confidence to make their own informed choice and planning in their own classrooms.

Peter King
July 1983

Acknowledgements

The author and publishers wish to thank Frank Dickens and the *Daily Express* for permission to reproduce the cartoon on page 88. The author wishes to thank all those teachers whose lessons are featured here, without whose help this book would not have been possible.

PART ONE
GENERAL CONSIDERATIONS

1

BASIC SKILLS
IN THE
ENGLISH CURRICULUM

Introduction

For nearly two decades, formal grammar and the accurate use of language have been anathema to most teachers of English in schools. In the mid-1960s creative writing replaced grammar as the popular vehicle for teaching the use of the English language. It was as though the master carpenters had decided to dispense with the teaching of essential skills and allowed their apprentices to create what they could by imagination alone. The apprentices would have learned nothing, and the consequences for children, forced to submit to this approach to teaching the craft of English, were hardly less disastrous.
(John Rae, 'The decline and fall of English Grammar', *Observer*, 7.2.82.)

This book is about the teaching of spelling, punctuation and grammar in secondary schools — what is often referred to as teaching the basic skills of English. The term 'basic skills', however, is a misnomer. Spelling and punctuation are relevant only to *written* English, which is itself derivative from spoken English. Furthermore, within English it is more important that children should have something worthwhile to write and should be able to express themselves effectively, than that their writing should be accurate in every minute detail. Most English teachers would feel that their main concerns are with *what* the pupil writes and *how* he expresses it, and one would not want to dissent from this view. Accuracy of spelling, punctuation and written grammar are surface skills, not basic skills.

The debate about the place which teaching these skills should occupy in the English curriculum is a perennial one, and one which, from time to time, surfaces in the press. John Rae's article initiated a spirited debate and brought fairly predictable replies, one, from a university lecturer supporting Dr Rae and bewailing the decline in 'standards':

> I have no doubt about the decline in the ability to write even 'fundamental' English. There has been an alarming — and still growing — proportion of students who haven't the slightest idea of what constitutes a sentence. The full stop, when used, is more an arbitrary and random indication of exhaustion than a form of punctuation.... It is sometimes easier to teach overseas students than British-born ones.

another strongly, not to say vituperatively, opposed:

> The article revealed his true self — a reactionary and limited thinker who repeats all the clichés of the uninformed and prejudiced about how children master language, contains not a single hard fact and ignores all the evidence.

Up to a point John Rae's analysis is correct. There has always been for English teachers a tension between helping children to write fluently, with good sense, excitement and conviction, and helping them to write 'correctly', to observe the conventions of written English. He is right in suggesting that, in the fifties and sixties, there was a move away from an emphasis on the mechanics of written English in the direction of a 'language through experience' approach. Symptomatic of this change was the appearance on the market of a new kind of English course book, following a thematic or 'topic' approach, providing source material (visual and literary) to stir children's imaginations and stimulate 'creative' writing. 'Growth through English' became the watchword of the day.

Dr Rae, however, is wrong in his diagnosis, suggesting that the change was due to a mood of self-indulgence and sentimental liberalism among English teachers. Rather it was, in part, a reaction against the stultifying effects of a 'basic skills' approach to English, with its emphasis on dull and repetitive exercises, taken largely out of context. And in part it derived from the accumulation of evidence about the futility of grammar teaching, and the exposure by linguists of its unscientific basis, confirming teachers' own experience that overemphasis on 'correctness' 'can dry up the flow of language and shackle creative and imaginative writing before it is under way' (Newsom Report, 1964).

The utilitarian mood of the late 1970s, however, saw a renewed concern with 'standards' in education, the initiation of wider public scrutiny of the curriculum, and the setting up of the APU to monitor national standards. Inevitably, perhaps, 'standards' in English teaching is commonly believed to refer to how well children can read and how accurately they can write. Employers, we are told, want school leavers who can spell correctly and who can write a grammatical and well-punctuated letter. So uncertainty about the role of the English teacher remains and we feel, perhaps guiltily, that we ought to spend more time teaching the mechanics of written English in our lessons.

Protagonists in the controversy, as the tone of the above letters makes clear, tend to see things in black and white — either basic skills are central to the English curriculum or they have no place at all — whereas the question is essentially one of their importance *relative* to other tasks of the English teacher. Of course we all want children to become fluent and flexible in their writing, to use their imaginations and develop their experience. Equally, of course, we would all like to help children spell accurately, punctuate well, and write grammatically. Both of these objectives are important for the pupil, and it could be argued that an English teacher who neglected either of them completely would be seriously failing his pupils. Nevertheless, many English teachers feel reluctant to spend time on the teaching of spelling, grammar and punctuation, believing that such time could more profitably be spent on other activities. Perhaps they feel time so occupied is largely wasted; children's own writing does not seem to improve as a direct result of such teaching, though they may become more adept at dictation, spelling tests, or language exercises. Perhaps some teachers believe that these matters can be left to themselves, that as children become more practised readers and writers their command of the basic skills will develop involuntarily and incidentally.

The rest of this book is devoted to examining how the basic skills develop in children, and to what extent they can be effectively taught in secondary schools. In this chapter we argue in more detail the case for teaching the basic skills and consider what 'correctness' in spelling, punctuation and grammar means.

Why teach spelling and punctuation?

The cases for teaching spelling and punctuation can be considered together. The most important reason is that poor spelling and punctuation interfere, to a greater or lesser degree, with the communication between writer and reader. There is nothing inherently 'right' or 'wrong' about the conventions of spelling and punctuation. Although there is a loose connection between spelling and pronunciation, and between punctuation and some of the features of spoken language (intonation, pauses, stress), essentially the conventions exist simply because, over a period of time, the literate community have come to an agreement about what constitutes the 'correct' conventions. It was not always so. In Shakespeare's time any spelling which approximated to the sound of a word was acceptable – over twenty different spellings of Shakespeare's own name exist. However, once conventions become stabilized, any departure from the 'correct' convention is likely to interfere with the smooth flow of reading. It is true that, if I write 'practice' instead of 'practise', you may not even notice the error, let alone find your reading impeded. And if I write 'eny diparcher frum the kurekt werdz', you can make out my meaning easily enough, but very likely you had to pause and puzzle out my intention. Punctuation differs slightly in that there is more scope for variations of style and personal preference – whether to use commas, for instance, or whether to use a colon rather than a dash earlier in this sentence. Usually, however, the scope for discretion is small, and a badly punctuated passage can be difficult to read, or even ambiguous, as in the headline 'Ban on strippers after stag party upsets vicar'.

So, accurate spelling and punctuation are important because otherwise the effectiveness of pupils' written work is impaired. Many children in secondary schools, however, will already be reasonably skilful spellers and punctuators, and their occasional mistakes will not seriously interfere with the communicative effectiveness of their writing. However, there is a second reason for teaching spelling and punctuation – a social one. Rightly or wrongly, good spelling and punctuation are regarded as desirable attainments, and a person who is prone to error may be regarded as 'uneducated' or 'ignorant'. Pupils in the top forms of secondary schools are well aware of the social stigma attached to poor spelling and punctuation, and, indeed, may well have developed rigid, defensive attitudes about their ability – 'I'm a rotten speller', 'I've never been able to punctuate', and, by inference, 'I never *will* be able to'. Clearly, a school which rates spelling and punctuation as of no importance is doing its pupils a disservice. Equally clearly, it is important for teachers to try to offer constructive help to pupils and not to create poor attitudes and lower motivation by negative measures such as scattering red ink all over exercise books, or informing children that their spelling/ punctuation is abysmal (they know that already). That Sandra has spelt 'allthough' wrongly for the third essay in succession is not a cause for moral indignation, though it may be a cause for querying one's own teaching methods.

Although spelling and punctuation matter for both social and communicative reasons, it is evident that accuracy is not *always* vital. In writing which is essentially private (as in letters between close friends), or writing for oneself (as when making notes for later use), the conventions can safely be disregarded. Also, when one is putting one's thoughts on paper for the first time, the ideas need to run uncluttered by worries about mechanical accuracy. The first draft of this chapter is full of crossings-out, false starts, and errors caused by the careless flow of composition. A writer may need to revise his or her work many times before arriving at a version fit to present to public gaze. So to expect children to write 'from cold' and produce straight off a polished version is to demand of them something which we do not often demand of ourselves. Children need the opportunity to scribble away 'carelessly' at their own rough drafts and, if necessary, to work at and revise their offerings before producing a final draft. Stressing mechanical accuracy at too early a stage will damage a child's confidence in his own writing skills and cause the well of inspiration to dry up. It follows, too, that teachers should think how they can provide genuine contexts for correctly presented written work. Wall displays, form magazines, pupil anthologies, letters to newspapers, are all contexts in which accurate spelling and punctuation are clearly seen to be important.

To argue that young people, when they leave school, should be able to spell and punctuate with reasonable accuracy, is to leave unanswered the questions of how this may be achieved and, indeed, whether these skills need to be specifically taught or whether they will somehow develop naturally as children get older. Since much of the rest of this book examines these questions, we simply state here our conviction that spelling and punctuation *can* be taught effectively and advocate that they *should* be taught in a consistent and systematic manner. However, instruction in the basic skills should not loom too large in the total English teaching programme. It is doubtful whether much class time can reasonably be allocated for this purpose in comparison with the other tasks which confront the English teacher. Rather, help for pupils to improve their spelling and punctuation needs to be integrated unobtrusively into the English programme, often alongside or incidental to other activities.

Why teach grammar?

The case for teaching grammar in secondary schools is both more complex and more controversial. Not only is a multiplicity of reasons put forward for the teaching of grammar, but there is no consensus about what 'teaching grammar' might mean. The aim of teaching spelling and punctuation is clear – to help children spell and punctuate correctly. The same aim can be offered for grammar teaching – to help children write correctly, though what 'correctly' means in this context is open to debate. But many other aims have been put forward: to help children write more effectively, to help them learn foreign languages, to give them an insight into the way language works, to equip them with a grammatical nomenclature which they will find useful, even that grammar is a unique discipline which 'trains the mind'. Compared with the mundane aim of teaching spelling and punctuation, we have a veritable peacock's tail of gaudy objectives. Corresponding to these different aims are different meanings attached to 'teaching grammar', ranging from a full-blown course of instruction in parts of speech, parsing and clause analysis, to a few incidental comments about 'use of adjectives' thrown out by the teacher when discussing, say, Lawrence's 'Snake'.

Considering first, then, how far it is necessary to teach children 'correct' grammar, there is one crucial difference between grammar and the other basic skills. Whereas there is no way in which children can have learned to spell and punctuate before they start school, by the age of 5 children have already mastered the main grammatical structures of the language and have a flexible command of the grammar of spoken English. How children do this remains something of a mystery, since it cannot be by the conscious understanding of grammar which often characterizes foreign language learning by older pupils. The American linguist Noam Chomsky argued that, such was the speed and quality of early grammar learning, it was necessary to postulate an innate capacity in human beings to learn grammar – an inborn 'language acquisition device'. Human beings are programmed to learn grammar; given an adequate language environment in the early years they acquire an amazing facility in handling the grammatical resources of their mother tongue.

Just as it makes prima facie sense to teach spelling and punctuation in schools, so it seems obvious nonsense to teach grammar. Why teach children something they already 'know' intuitively? But what children know, what they personally operate, is literally the grammar of their mother tongue, the grammar of spoken English and, moreover, of a particular variety of spoken English. There are many varieties of spoken English – regional (dialect), socio-economic, ethnic, occupational, peer-group. Each variety will have its own grammatical variants on 'standard' English. Furthermore, the grammar of spoken English differs from the grammar of written English, and written English itself has many grammatical styles ranging from the very informal style of intimate correspondence to the convoluted style of legal documents. What teaching 'correct' grammar really means is teaching the grammar of formal written English. This is not really a matter of absolute correctness but of appropriateness, teaching the usage appropriate to a particular context. It is not, in principle, different from pupils modifying a broad regional accent in, say, a formal interview, or persuading a child to write 'The teacher would not countenance my misbehaviour and ejected me from the classroom' instead of 'The teacher wouldn't put up with me messing about and kicked me out of the classroom'. A pupil who writes 'He didn't ought to do it' is not writing ungrammatically – this is fully comprehensible, is a perfectly acceptable colloquial form and, indeed, is acceptable in certain written contexts. The usage is, however, unacceptable in formal written English, but this is essentially a problem of appropriateness and not of correctness. The general teaching strategy to be adopted, then, is to widen the pupil's linguistic repertoire and increase his ability to handle a variety of language contexts (technically, to make him competent in a range of 'registers'), and not to attack his own grammatical usages as somehow 'wrong' or 'incorrect'. What part, if any, grammar teaching has in this will be taken up in Chapter 4.

Of the other justifications for grammar teaching, some may be readily disposed of. Chief among these is the myth that teaching grammar helps pupils to write more effectively. Decades of research[1] have shown that there is *no* detectable spin-off from grammar teaching in pupils' own writing. Children already 'know' intuitively how to generate grammatical sentences, and the way to release this underlying competence is to provide appropriate contexts for writing. No amount of clause analysis, for instance, will help pupils to link their own sentences more effectively, any more than a knowledge of physics makes one a more skilful car driver. And this holds whatever the grammatical model being employed; teachers should beware the peddler of the old discredited formal grammar in new transformational or structural bottles. It won't work. What *may* work, of course, is practice in using certain kinds of grammatical structure. Some of the alleged benefits of grammar teaching turn out to be due entirely to systematic, structured practice and not at all to the grammatical edifice built on it. English teachers are wasting their time if they teach grammar in the hope that it will improve the quality of their pupils' writing.

Another claim that has no validity is that grammar teaching 'trains the mind'. The argument seems to be that grammar is especially logical, and study of it a valuable intellectual discipline. In fact, the grammar of English is often illogical, or at best a compromise among conflicting rules and their exceptions which has developed piecemeal over the centuries. It may be partly for this reason that English grammar was for so long distorted to fit the mould of Latin grammar which, as a dead language, was felt perhaps to be more logical.

Another aim put forward for grammar teaching is that it helps in the learning of foreign languages. An English syllabus in use in the early 1960s had, under the heading of grammar:

Week 1 The nominative case
Week 2 The accusative case
Week 3 The vocative case

The reason was not far to seek; in the Latin syllabus, nominative, vocative and accusative cases were being taught in the first three weeks. The futility of this exercise should be apparent. English is not primarily an inflected language, only vestigial traces of cases survive, and even these are often confused and, therefore, on the way out (who/whom, between you and I, the misused apostrophe). This was really an excuse to teach Latin through the English syllabus. And even when there is an apparently better match between the grammars of two different languages, the differences will be sufficient to make comparison confusing. Modern language teachers are best advised to teach the grammar of their language *through* that language. It is no part of the English teacher's task to teach grammar for that purpose.

However, it may undeniably be useful for pupils to have some acquaintance with grammatical nomenclature. The French teacher's task will be easier if pupils know roughly what terms like 'subject', 'object', 'noun', 'verb', 'preposition' refer to. The English teacher, too, *may* find it useful to use grammatical terms on occasion. For instance, in discussing a passage of literature, or in helping children with their written work, it can be a convenient shorthand to be able to use terms such as 'phrases', 'conjunctions', 'adjectives'. It might even be argued that an educated person should have some understanding of basic grammatical categories as part of his general knowledge. How such an understanding might be encouraged within an English programme will be taken up in Chapter 4.

The final and most persuasive (though not the most widely raised) argument for teaching grammar is that language study is a valuable activity in its own right. Language is an important part of our culture, it is argued; indeed, language is what distinguishes us as a species. Linguistic study, therefore, should be a central part of education, and an insight into how grammar functions should be a central part of that study. Stated thus, it is difficult not to sympathize with this view. Indeed, fostering a lively and intelligent interest in the mother tongue in all its aspects could properly be seen as a major concern of the English teacher. However, one would want to enter an important caveat about grammar teaching which, properly conceived of, is a rather difficult and abstract pursuit. We all know intuitively the grammar of our mother tongue; to stand back from our own thought processes and to make explicit the patterns and rules which govern them demands a level of reasoning which develops in most children only in mid-adolescence. Only from the third and fourth forms onwards, and then only with the most able pupils, will grammatical study, as an exercise in its own right, have the kind of appeal which might justify its inclusion in the syllabus. Although many opportunities will arise for the English teacher to offer incidental insights into grammatical structure, he need not have a guilty conscience if he *never* undertakes any formal, class-based grammatical analysis.

Over the last twenty years, the formal teaching of grammar in a systematic way has disappeared from most of our secondary schools. Formal grammar exercises no longer appear on examination papers or figure prominently in school syllabuses. The reasons are clear: on the one hand, such teaching has no effect on pupils' writing (except, perhaps, the deleterious effect of giving them one more thing to worry about); on the other hand, learning grammar tends to be difficult, abstract and pointless for all but a few able pupils. One consequence of the demise of grammar teaching has been that many English teachers now entering schools have not themselves undergone a course in grammar. Some may have taken linguistic courses at university, or have looked briefly at grammar teaching on their certificate courses, but many young English teachers will be ill-equipped to teach grammar, even if they wanted to. While one would not want to press grammar teaching in schools, a strong case can be made out for all prospective English teachers taking a course in linguistics which would include some basic study of the grammar of English and techniques of grammatical investigation.

References

1.   Summarized in A. Wilkinson, *The Foundations of Language* (Oxford, Oxford University Press, 1971), pp. 32–5.

2

PROBLEMS IN LEARNING TO SPELL

Learned or taught?

Spelling has to be learned. However natural it seems for people who are good spellers, all of us, at some time in our lives, have had to learn to spell. We are reminded of this whenever we come across a word we have not written before; unless the spelling conforms to regular phonic rules, we must make a guess — a guess admittedly helped by all sorts of linguistic clues, but none the less a guess which may be wrong. Only an avid reader of gardening books is like to get 'eschscholtzia' right at the first time of asking.

However, to say that spelling has to be learned does not necessarily imply that it has to be taught. For many years a fierce debate raged over whether spelling was taught, or whether it was 'caught', that is, learned incidentally by children alongside their learning to read and write. There is no doubt that many children *do* learn to spell with a minimum of overt teaching. These are often children who are blessed in other ways: children of above average intelligence and linguistic skills, children who read fluently, have a good vocabulary, and write speedily and with ease. Accurate spelling may be one manifestation of a general proficiency in language. At the same time, it is clear that many children do *not* 'catch' spelling in this kind of way. Their written work is profusely littered with spelling errors, and hopes that they will be cured 'in time' turn out to be unfounded. While some of these poor spellers may well experience problems in reading and writing, this is by no means always the case. Some of the very fastest adult readers are also poor spellers, and it is not unknown for English teachers themselves to be fallible in this respect.

It is worth examining more closely the connection between reading and spelling, for it is sometimes assumed that improving reading skills will automatically improve spelling, and for this reason teachers need not bother with the direct teaching of spelling. It is certainly true that it is while we are reading that we encounter new words which we will later need to spell; however, only a small proportion of spellings are incidentally 'picked up' while reading, and then more readily by people who are already good spellers. It is also true that both reading and spelling involve the same kind of skills, analytic, visual, auditory and linguistic, but they make use of these skills in somewhat different ways. Finally, there is evidence to suggest that children who have been taught to read in different ways make different kinds of spelling mistake.[1] Teachers who, during the early stages of teaching reading, direct children's attention to the internal structure of words, to similar patterns among groups of words, and to difficult spots in words, will help to build up an intuitive 'feel' for the structures of English spelling.

The basic ground-rules of both reading and spelling rest upon the relationship between significant sounds (phonemes) and written forms (graphemes). In reading, we decode the written word into sound and meaning. In spelling we encode sounds into a written form. The latter is often a more problematic and ambiguous process. In reading, where a grapheme may have a number of possible phonemic equivalents, the context usually indicates clearly which is correct. How, for instance, should one read '-ough'? We don't know, but put it in context and usually we will get it right. 'The farmer drove his pl*ough* thr*ough* the gate and over the r*ough* ground.' In spelling, we have no such contextual clues. If a child needs to *write* a word *right*, he has no easy way of choosing between the alternatives. And this is true of some of the commonest words in the language; 'there' and 'their' are both fairly unusual graphemic representations of the vowel sound – 'thear', 'thair' or 'thare' would be much more likely. One way or another we have simply to learn the correct spellings.

Processes of spelling

What, then, are the processes involved in spelling a word? First, we may sound the word to ourselves. Secondly, we may break the word down into its constituent parts – syllables and ultimately sounds (phonemes). Thirdly, we may visualize the written form of the constituent parts, and associate written letters (graphemes) with them. Fourthly, when alternative graphemes are possible we need to decide amongst them. Fifthly we may visualize the whole word to see if it 'looks' right. Finally we apply our motor skills and write the word down. Of course, for a practised speller the total process has become so habitual that he may move straight from the sound of the word to writing and the intermediate steps are omitted, just as a confident touch-typist is no longer aware of the struggles and stages through which she attained mastery of the keyboard.

It follows that poor spelling may stem from many causes. If a child has weak auditory skills he may not be able to represent the sound of a word to himself, or analyse it into its constituent parts. Such a child will make 'unphonetic' errors ('rail' for 'really', 'palorl' for 'parallel') and may well also be experiencing difficulty with his reading. A child may not be able to associate sounds with letters, though this will be rare in children of secondary school age. A child may have a poor visual memory, so that he can make the phoneme–grapheme link, but cannot visualize how the word should 'look'. This will result in 'phonetic' misspellings ('lonley', 'opund'), and will not affect his reading. A child may not know how to choose among alternative graphemes, or chooses wrongly. The vast majority of spelling mistakes among adults and older children who have adequate auditory and visual memory are of this kind. I give a sample from two short essays written by a university student (who also shows signs of poor visual memory): wasteage, authentisity, seperate, obsticals, nobel, surpress, highten, remedie, devision, explaination, concidering, liturature, dicipline, conciousness, privilaged, willful, idealogies. What characterizes these errors is that they are, in the main, intelligent guesses but they happen to be wrong. Finally, a child may experience motor problems in actually writing the word down; we all make 'slips of the pen' from time to time, but for some children the mechanical process of writing may present unusual difficulty.

The upshot of this is that a secondary school teacher will be faced, especially in a mixed-ability class, with children who vary greatly in their spelling competencies. At one extreme will be children who are very proficient spellers, and who know how to verify the spelling of a word if they are unsure. At the other extreme may be children who are very poor readers and for whom simply getting something down on paper presents sufficient difficulty without worrying about the spelling. In between will be children with a range of spelling problems stemming from a variety of causes. As well as the auditory, visual and motor problems already discussed, some children may have developed bad spelling habits because of inefficient teaching previously; yet others may have become so depressed by past failure that they have ceased to believe they can improve their spelling and have given up trying.

In general terms, the teacher of spelling will try to do three things. First, he will direct children's attention to the appearance, sound and structure of words, and to regularities among words, and so help them to acquire a 'feel' for the underlying 'rules' of spelling. Secondly, he will give children lots of practice, so that good spelling becomes automatic and habitual. He will help them to co-ordinate sound, appearance and motor activity when learning to spell, and will ensure they acquire good learning techniques and strategies. Thirdly, he will assist them to develop strategies for discovering correct spellings when they are in doubt.

However, the wide individual differences among children's spelling competencies and the underlying causes of their problems imply that, in any particular class, children's needs will be very different. It follows that teaching spelling to a whole class will seldom be justified; effective spelling teaching must be geared to the needs of individual pupils. Word lists for spelling, for instance, should be derived from the pupils' own written work, and often it will be more appropriate for each pupil to build up and learn his own lists. At one extreme it is pointless to emphasize spelling with a child who can scarcely read; at the other extreme, time spent on spelling is wasted on a child who can already spell proficiently.

Since the causes of poor spelling are so varied, teachers need to use, and encourage children to use themselves, a variety of strategies. Consider a misspelling such as 'seperate'. It may be that a child will be helped by repeatedly looking at the word, attempting to visualize it, and focusing on the difficult spot – sepArate; it may be that sounding the word will be the best strategy, emphasizing the troublesome syllable – se-PAR-ate; or it may be that the child will benefit from repeatedly copying or tracing the word with the pen or finger, so forming the correct motor habit. One or more of these or other strategies may work with different pupils. Over and above this a teacher has to consider how best to motivat pupils, to get them to care about and take trouble over their spelling without their becoming obsessively concerned to the detriment of their writing. Again, the teacher needs at his command a variety of resources to develop good attitudes and habits in pupils.

Are there rules?

Of central importance to learning spelling is the extent to which English spelling may be regarded as governed by rules and regularities. In terms of spelling regularity, written languages lie along a continuum from complete phoneme–grapheme correspondence to complete idiographic representation. In the first case (so-called 'phonetic' alphabets) each sound in the language would be represented by one written character, and each character would stand for one sound only. In theory, the spelling of any word would be immediately deducible from its pronunciation, once the basic rules had been learned. The second case of idiographic representation (as in classical Chinese) implies that each word has its own written character, and learning to write is a matter of learning the thousands of symbols for the different words of a language.

Whereabouts does English fall on this continuum? Clearly English has, in principle, a phonemic writing system. The written characters do, most of the time, either singly or in combination, have a close relationship to the sounds of words. Indeed, before spelling became crystallized, any adequate graphemic equivalent was acceptable (Shakspear, Shekespere, etc.), and although we may hold all sorts of attitudes towards someone who writes 'sufishunt', we understand perfectly well what is intended. Even today there are a few words with legitimate alternative spellings – 'grey' or 'gray', 'judgement' or 'judgment', 'criticise' or 'criticize', and, of course, there are transatlantic variants such as center, defense, honor, program.

However, although written English is in principle phonemic, such is the complex history of English orthography that, in practice, there are few regularities. Early reading schemes often concentrate on graphemically regular words of the 'cat, sat, mat' variety, but such schemes seem very artificial, since so many of the commonest English words have unusual spellings.

It is rare in English for one grapheme to represent just one phoneme, and vice versa. Consonants are the most regular. Thus, written 'b' usually stands for spoken 'b' (though this will not help a child to distinguish 'rabbit' from 'habit'; or to pronounce 'lamb', 'doubtful'), and 'sh' nearly always represents the same phoneme (but note 'shear' and 'mishear'). Although, as we have seen, contextual clues make it easier to resolve uncertainty when reading, there may, when spelling, be no obvious clues for deciding which of several competing graphemes is correct. For instance, the phoneme 'ks' is represented variously in bo*x*, so*cks*, picni*cs*, cor*ks*, a*cc*ident, e*xc*essive. And if consonants provide snares and brambles for the unwary speller, the English vowel system is a veritable jungle. Largely for historical reasons, there is a complete lack of phoneme–grapheme correspondence for vowels. Thus written 'a' may stand singly for several sounds (fat, father, wash, water, above, amoral), and, in combination with other letters, for many more; more seriously as far as spelling is concerned, one vowel sound may be written in many ways. So we have pear/pair/pare (but also their/there/they're), two/to/too (but tutu).

Faced with this diversity in phoneme–grapheme relationships, the task of the speller is clear; provided he has learned the basic regularities (and by the time they start secondary school most children will have acquired this knowledge intuitively, through their reading, if not through formal teaching of spelling), how is he to decide among competing possible spellings? By 'decide' is meant here 'choose quickly and maybe intuitively', since to stop and think about a spelling slows down the flow of writing. What clues does a good speller use to get words right most of the time?

Although English spelling often seems arbitrary, it is shaped by a number of linguistic and historical principles of which good spellers seem to have developed an intuitive understanding. Indeed, some linguists talk about the 'deep structure' of English spelling. It is like a game governed by complex and interlocking rules; it is not easy to formulate which rules will operate in a particular situation, but if you are a sophisticated player, you come up with the right answer most of the time. Consider, for instance, the old chestnut that 'fish' might equally well be spelt 'ghoti' ('gh' as in 'cough', 'o' as in women' and 'ti' as in 'station'). A good speller knows that this is not so. In the first place he is guided by probabilities. He knows that 'o' and 'gh' are very rare representations of the i and f sounds, and if in doubt will plump for the commoner 'i' and 'f'. Secondly, he knows not just about probabilities but about sequential and positional probabilities. Thus 'gh' never spells 'f' at the beginning of words and 'ti' never spells 'sh' at the end. Going back to the earlier example of the 'ks' sound, a good speller will know that words do not end in 'cc' or 'xc' and that 'cks' is rare in medial positions. Thirdly, he will have some understanding of the structure of words. 'Picnics' and 'socks' will be correctly spelt because they are plural forms of picnic and sock, but 'bocks' or 'bocs' would imply something called a 'bock' or 'boc'. He will be able to break words down into their constituent parts, and will have no problems with 'sincere-ly', 'mis-spell', 'dis-appear'. Fourthly, he will be able to form analogies and so develop certain 'rules of thumb' even if these are not specifically formulated. So 'comical', 'practical', 'electrical' produce 'comically', 'practically', 'electrically' (not 'comicly', 'electricly'), and by analogy 'realistically' (though there is no stem 'realistical'). But he will need to remember the exceptions and may well get 'publicly' wrong. Fifthly, the origins of words often give a clue to their spelling, and though Latin is less often taught nowadays, a good speller has acquired incidentally quite a sensitive understanding of etymology. So, he groups together 'cede', 'recede', 'secede', 'concede', 'precede', though he will need to remember 'proceed', 'exceed', 'succeed' as a separate group. A good speller, then, will have a wealth of internalized knowledge about English spelling, much of it 'picked up' incidentally, but some of it perhaps fostered by the systematic efforts of teachers. This is what Peters calls the paradox of spelling – 'Spelling is ultimately not a rational activity, yet one that can be taught by rational methods' (M. L. Peters, *Success in Spelling*, p. 37).

This raises the controversial question of spelling rules, such as 'i before e except after c'. The purpose of such rules is to help us when we are not sure how a word should be spelt. As such, their usefulness is limited, since we cannot keep stopping every few seconds to summon up the appropriate rule. Nevertheless, rules may be a valuable standby, especially for competent spellers who have persistent blind-spots. To be really useful, a rule should be simple to understand and remember, cover a worthwhile number of cases, and have few exceptions. On the face of it, our 'i before e' rule meets these criteria. Since it rhymes, it is easy to remember. A few illustrative examples (receive/believe) should enable children to understand it. However, the rule is incomplete as it stands; it requires the addition of 'when the sound is -ee-', to eliminate 'rein, heir, height' and similar words. And then, one needs to remember the common exceptions – seize, counterfeit, protein. So even this apparently simple rule turns out to be quite complicated. Indeed, for many children the learning of formal rules will be a waste of time, especially when the rule requires a complex feat of memorization in itself or is couched in language which contains unfamiliar jargon. For instance, do you know the rule which helps you to determine whether the correct spelling is 'benefiting', or 'benefitting'? It runs like this: 'When a suffix beginning with a vowel is added to a word ending in a consonant, the final consonant is doubled if the stress falls on the syllable immediately preceding the consonant. 'If you can unravel that, it points to 'bénefiting' as the correct spelling, but you might be forgiven for remembering simply that it was different from 'fitting', or using a pair like 'reférred/réference' to help you in similar cases.

Helping children to spell

Using spelling rules is just one of a number of strategies that can be used when we are unsure of a word's spelling. Teachers can help children to develop these strategies. All children, for instance, should learn how to use a dictionary to verify spellings. They can be encouraged to keep their own personal 'dictionaries' of words they get wrong, not just for consultation, but also for learning as part of an individual spelling programme. Some children benefit from visual strategies, such as writing out different spellings and seeing which 'looks' right, others prefer auditory strategies such as misemphasizing the pronunciation of a word so as to pinpoint its spelling ('embarrassment' with a rolled 'r', 'harássment' with the Americanized stress). Even the best spellers get words wrong occasionally and need ways of checking on their spelling. It will do no harm if a teacher makes the odd mistake himself; this could provide the starting-point for a fruitful discussion with pupils.

For, in the last resort, English spelling is arbitrary and unpredictable. When all the spelling rules and regulations have been taken into account, a great many English words, among them some of the commonest, have simply to be learned. A computer has been programmed with 300 spelling rules, but can still spell correctly under half the words in its language sample, and would be outspelled by the average 10-year-old. As one writer puts it: 'Average spellers spell by rule, good spellers spell by rote.'

As in all learning, two features are of cardinal importance – practice and motivation. The teacher must provide frequent opportunities and incentives for children to develop good learning habits, so that they can practise their spellings and receive assurance that they are improving, and must create a climate in which children want to improve their spelling, believe they *can* make progress, and are willing to invest time and trouble in doing so. Too often the way in which pupils' work is received, corrected and commented on, and the way in which spelling instruction is conducted through lists, tests and formal dictation, serve only to create negative attitudes towards spelling and poor self-concepts amongst the weaker spellers. Spelling is something teachers and pupils can work at together, in partnership. As Mike Torbe puts it: 'The teacher's job is not to correct mistakes the pupil has already made, but to help him not to make that mistake next time' (M. Torbe, *Teaching Spelling*, p. 12).

Finally, to repeat the caveat made earlier: keep a sense of proportion about spelling. The best classrooms are those where pupils write freely and with confidence. Spelling should never be the main concern of an English teacher nor the chief worry of a pupil. However, in a classroom where the priorities of English teaching are observed, there is no reason why a systematic and effective spelling policy should not be pursued. Indeed, if his pupils are not improving their spelling, an English teacher is failing in a small part of his duty.

References

1. See, for instance, M. L. Peters, *Success in Spelling* (Cambridge, Cambridge Institute of Education, 1970), Chapter 5.

3

TEACHING PUNCTUATION

Individual teaching

A small survey carried out recently in secondary schools in the East Midlands revealed a surprising degree of unanimity about the teaching of punctuation. Whereas the formal teaching of grammar was virtually non-existent, and the teaching of spelling rather haphazard – left often to the discretion of individual teachers – there appeared to be general agreement that punctuation needed to be taught systematically, at any rate in the early years of secondary school. Lessons or parts of lessons were regularly given over to instruction in the commonest punctuation marks: full stops and capital letters, commas, apostrophes, and punctuation of direct speech.

Like spelling, punctuation clearly has to be learned; it is an offshoot of literacy and has no direct counterpart in spoken language. At the same time it cannot be assumed that punctuation will be 'picked up' as children learn to read. While some of the more linguistically gifted children may incidentally acquire a good deal, other children plainly do not, and it would seem common sense to point out to all pupils the main conventions of punctuation and to give them punctuation practice. And yet, punctuation skills, practised in isolation, have very little effect on pupils' own written work. All teachers must have come across the pupil who completes perfectly the exercise on punctuating direct speech, yet whose 'knowledge' seems to fly out of the window when it comes to using direct speech in his own compositions. In higher education one finds students who have, presumably, over the years been taught many times the use of the apostrophe yet who have not the slightest idea when to use it themselves, and either miss it out altogether or scatter it like confetti all over their work.

As with spelling, instruction by itself is not enough. Children must *want* to punctuate correctly, must understand the reason for a particular use of punctuation, and above all must practise it in connection with their own written work. It follows that the most helpful kind of work will be undertaken individually. A teacher, when marking work, may wish to indicate what important errors are being made or what punctuation resources are not being exploited, discuss these with individual pupils and give them appropriate practice. Pupils may keep punctuation notebooks, or records of correct/incorrect usage in the back of their exercise books, which they can refer to when they are redrafting their written work for formal presentation.

Class teaching

Nevertheless, there are occasions when teachers may want to spend ten minutes or so of class time dealing with punctuation. Not all punctuation marks are alike. Some, such as the full-stop, question-mark, comma, semi-colon, colon, dashes, brackets have to do with the structure of the sentence, and correct use of them depends, in part, on the child's grasp of variations in sentence structure and the relationships among different parts of the sentence. Very often one finds an improvement in sentence punctuation as the child's syntactic performance improves; certainly there seems little point teaching the 'correct' use of commas to a pupil who has difficulty even in recognizing what is a 'proper' sentence. Other punctuation marks, however, seem to be mere ortho- graphic conventions: capital letters (especially to indicate proper nouns), the apostrophe in both its uses, full-stops for abbreviations, the hyphen, inverted commas and all the other conventions to do with direct speech. It is difficult to see how a child can learn to use these unless he is taught. Certainly there is little excuse for a case like the able 13-year-old who realized for the first time that an apostrophe had to be used with inanimate objects (the book's cover) and not just animate creatures (John's book, the dog's tail) – no one had ever told him previously. So, some instruction in punctuation will need to be given, and class instruction will sometimes seem the most economical way. Occasionally, too, practice exercises may be set or pieces of written work with particular punctuation marks in mind ('I'm going to pay special attention to how you set out the conversation in your story'). The main attention, however, should always be to the problems of individual pupils, and to the effective use of punctuation in their own written work.

Class teaching of punctuation needs relating to the ability of the class and to their previous knowledge. For instance, the more sophisticated punctuation marks, such as semi-colon or colon, are worth discussing only with a group who already have a sound command of more basic marks such as the comma and full-stop. When pupils arrive at secondary school they will probably have already experienced some instruction in punctuation at primary school: certainly punctuation of sentences, probably something on direct speech, perhaps instruction in commas and apostrophe. (This last is probably undertaken too early; much of the later confusion about the apostrophe stems from its being taught to children who are unable to understand its use – thereafter it remains a mysterious symbol whose correct deployment depends on good luck rather than judgement.) The first-year teacher will need to take account of and perhaps 'pull together' the different punctuation experiences of his pupils.

As well as the timing of punctuation teaching, sequencing needs to be considered. Some punctuation conventions are complex and need breaking down into small steps, presented one at a time, perhaps at intervals. The conventions of direct speech are a good instance of this. At first, children should practise using the inverted commas to enclose the words actually spoken without worrying too much about other punctuation marks in speech. Rather than teaching punctuation of direct speech in one go, we would recommend coming back to the topic at intervals throughout the secondary course, continually elaborating and building upon what has previously been learned. Similarly, it is a mistake to introduce both uses of the apostrophe together. They should be taught separately (to avoid confusion), gradually (taking one point at a time), and only when both usages are firmly grounded should they be compared, even though there is a historical connection between the two uses. This use of a 'spiral' curriculum to teach punctuation is further illustrated in Chapter 6.

Incidental teaching

As well as individual and class teaching of punctuation, the opportunity will sometimes arise to raise punctuation matters incidentally during the English lesson. Occasionally the teacher may wish to comment on a particular use of punctuation in a novel which is being read. Sometimes punctuation is crucial to the interpretation of a poem. For instance, reading T. S. Eliot's 'Journey of the Magi' with older pupils

But there was no information, and so we continued
And arrived at evening, not a moment too soon
Finding the place; it was (you may say) satisfactory.

All this was a long time ago, I remember,
And I would do it again, but set down
This set down
This: were we led all that way for
Birth or Death?

a teacher might well ask why the author has chosen to use brackets in line 3, or has not used a comma after 'this' in line 6. (How should this line be read?) Similarly, when dialogue occurs in a class novel, the teacher may ask how a particular speech should be read, and how we, the readers, know that.

In fact, stressing the connection between punctuation and speech is one of the most powerful ways of impressing on pupils the importance of punctuation and making them aware of its resources. Punctuation is a major way (often the only way) of indicating in writing features of the spoken language such as intonation, pitch, stress, pauses, juncture, even gesture and other non-verbal features, and of hinting at mood, intention, and tone. Ways in which this can be brought home to pupils are discussed in Chapter 6.

Punctuation and meaning

The other main purpose of punctuation is, of course, to clarify the meaning and assist reading. Getting children to read passages without punctuation makes the point readily enough; indeed, getting them to read back their own poorly punctuated work is a useful teaching strategy. Or they might be asked to use punctuation to clarify ambiguous sentences, or to distinguish between pairs like 'The boys who were late were punished'/'The boys, who were late, were punished'.

When teaching punctuation it is desirable to stress the resources of punctuation rather than narrow concerns of correctness. For while some usages are undeniably incorrect, much punctuation is essentially a matter of style, for instance many uses of the comma, or choice among different punctuation marks. Punctuation is best regarded as a way of helping us to write more effectively. We could with profit encourage children in their 'creative' writing to be more creative in their use of punctuation marks, including such typographical features as underlining, capitalization, layout and italics. The essential question to ask is 'Does it help the communication?' After all, great writers are often idiosyncratic in their punctuation. It is a great pity Kafka did not know how to write 'proper' sentences:

> But there was a time when he turned up too frequently for my taste, I told him so, we fell into conversation, I was curious to know how he could keep himself going entirely by his painting, and I discovered to my astonishment that he really earned his living as a portrait-painter.
> (F. Kafka, *The Trial*. Quoted in S. Cook, 'The Rise of the Comma', *Eng. in Ed.*, 6.1.1972.)

4

THE PLACE OF GRAMMAR

The development of children's grammar

Teaching grammar differs in one crucial respect from teaching spelling or punctuation. By the time they start school, children already have an intuitive mastery of all the major structures of English grammar, sufficient for the linguistic demands of their everyday life. What they can not yet do, of course, is translate into writing this basic grammatical competence in the spoken language. This is not just a matter of learning the physical skills of handwriting, and conventional representations of spelling and punctuation, but of mastering the different registers of written English, and learning to operate under the psychological constraints of writing, with its requirement of explicit and elaborated communication.

The development of children's grammar in the early years of schooling is well-documented. From the beginning, children are manifestly native English writers. They do not make the kinds of structural errors which non-native English speakers might make. They have a basic command of all the grammatical resources. What we find is a progressive development in the complexity and flexibility of their writing. As children grow older they tend to use longer and more grammatically complex sentences. The ubiquitous 'and' of the 8-year-old comes to be replaced by more varied and subtle ways of connecting sentences. The child in the early years of secondary school uses a wide range of subordinate clauses, sometimes in a rather cumbersome way. As he moves up the school so he adopts increasingly the more sophisticated 'embedding' devices of the adult writer. This development seems to take place naturally, quite without the assistance of any systematic grammar teaching. Partly the development seems to be linked to the general conceptual growth of children. For instance, there seems a definite order to the appearance of adverbial clauses in children's writing: firstly we have the widespread use of clauses of time (when, while, until, etc.), followed by reason, condition and place, then result and manner, and last of all concession, which is rare in the writing of junior school children.[1] Research has shown that many junior school children do not fully grasp the meaning implied by the use of 'although'. ('I enjoyed my holiday although the weather was fine' is a typical misunderstanding.) Similarly a development in the tentativeness of children's writing, the growing use of auxiliary verbs like may/might/should/can/ought to/must and conditional structures, may parallel a cognitive development in the direction of hypothesizing and making suppositions. What is clear is that writing ability develops as children are called upon to realize their linguistic competence in more and more varied and demanding writing tasks. Grammar teaching is at best irrelevant, at worst distracting.

Teaching 'correct' written English

This is the kind of grammar teaching that approximates most closely to the teaching of spelling and punctuation – it is a matter of helping children to use the grammatical forms conventionally agreed upon for writing. Unlike spelling and punctuation, however, one grammatical form has to be adopted in preference to an alternative form which the child already employs, quite appropriately, in other circumstances. Grammatical explanations, therefore, are really beside the point. Suppose a child writes: 'We was stood on the corner.' One might attempt a grammatical explanation along these lines: '"We" is plural, so the plural form "were" must be used; the verb "to be" takes the present participle after it, so "standing" should be used.' A linguistically sophisticated pupil might reply: 'You must be speaking a different language. In English, verbs in the first person have the same singular and plural ("I said/we said") – so why do you want to make an exception of "was"? And verbs expressing a state or position use the past participle – "He was sat on the chair", "The man was laid on the floor", "She was knelt by the door". If you say, "We were standing on the corner" round our way, you'll just get laughed at.' To this kind of grammatical disputation there is no end. Why not come clean and say: 'In writing, this usage is preferred to that'? Even though what children *write* may be wildly inappropriate, they seldom *speak* grammatical nonsense. And it is important not to attack the child's spoken language as being in some way 'inferior' or 'wrong', otherwise we cut him off from one of the most important tools of learning, his own spoken language.

In fact, persuading children to adopt different forms for written work is not, in principle, very difficult. From very early days in school children accept that writing has different conventions from speech. This is apparent to them both from learning to read, and their early struggles to write. As the APU survey makes clear, by the time they start secondary school most children (over 95 per cent) have a reasonable mastery of the grammatical conventions of written English, and some awareness of the need to provide stylistically appropriate writing. As they move through secondary school, they will extend the range of written registers in which they are proficient, and help with grammar is best seen as part of the teacher's attempt to increase the child's over-all linguistic mastery. 'How can you write what you want to write more effectively?' is the approach likely to bring about more flexible grammatical use. The APU report found that the basic grammatical conventions had been well mastered by nearly all 15-year-olds and that 'Weak writing was more likely to be found inadequate in terms of content and style than in relation to grammatical or orthographical conventions'.[2]

If a child is making persistent grammatical errors, or occasional grammatical errors which the teacher judges to be important, then these are best dealt with on an individual basis, the preferred form being indicated and the child encouraged to practise it, if necessary. The teacher, while marking, may decide that an error is sufficiently widespread to warrant class attention. Occasional class discussion of pupil errors may be valuable, provided it is presented as a discussion of conventions and not rigid laws. A too prescriptive approach leads, as one writer expressed it, 'to an impression of English language as being full of pitfalls for the unwary which only unremitting vigilance can avoid'.

Sometimes, although 'errors' are really errors of usage rather than grammar, a grammatical explanation may help the child to see the point of the correction and to remember it. For instance, a child who writes 'Everyone had forgotten their books' may find an explanation in terms of agreement of number helpful. But this example brings us up against one of the major stumbling blocks to teaching 'correct grammar' in schools. While most proficient writers agree in 99 per cent of cases on what constitutes 'good' English, the remaining 1 per cent of cases represent areas of major disagreement – and these are just the disputed usages which comprise the backbone of 'school grammar'. The boundary between 'correct' and 'incorrect' is *not* clear-cut, and there is often no clear majority in favour of preferring one form to another. If you want to start a heated argument among educated people, try asking them about the acceptability of the following, in spoken and written English:

'He is much admired.'
'Neither he nor I want to go.'
'It's me.'
'Chalk is different both to cheese and chutney.'
  (What do they think the 'error' is here?)
'Tom and myself play chess every Friday.'

This is not simply a matter of determining what is or is not actual usage, but also of taking into account what is socially accepted usage. And here schools must bear a heavy burden of responsibility for perpetuating usages which are moribund in normal written English. Many of the shibboleths of correctness beloved by English teachers in the past were completely arbitrary prescriptions, originally capriciously selected by some self-appointed guardian of the English language, and elevated to the status of a fixed standard of 'correctness'. Often these were based on a misguided analogy with Latin grammar ('It's I', you mustn't end a sentence with a preposition), or on some quaint view of logic, as in the embargo on a double negative – this despite the fact that the double negative in the sense of a very intensive negative has a respectable history, going back at least to Chaucer, that some other languages *do* use a double negative in this sense, and that two negatives do *not* make a positive, in language at any rate. ('I don't care about not winning' does *not* mean 'I care about winning' – rather the opposite.) Hunting for many of these 'errors' in children's writing is mere 'nit-picking', with no justification either in history or in current usage. Many of the so-called 'common errors' are either not common or else not errors. We all have our own particular shibboleths – I confess to 'due to/owing to', which must be about the most illogical and unjustifiable 'rule' ever foisted on children – and the English teacher would do well to take a self-denying ordinance about his own pet hates. The only authority is usage, and other authorities should be treated with scepticism. Even Fowler was described by one critic as 'a set of prejudices erected into a system'.[3] The moral for the English teacher is clear: if you must correct grammatical errors in pupils' work, make sure that the form you are recommending really is widely accepted correct usage; where two usages compete, be aware that one does not automatically have to be right and the other wrong; above all, avoid conveying the impression that the pupils' usages are somehow 'wrong' or 'inferior' rather than just inappropriate.

Sometimes, of course, there really will be grammatical errors. Usually these will be due to careless slips, for native-born English speakers hardly ever make totally unacceptable errors of the kind made by foreign speakers: 'I am staying here since three years, and I am very much liking your beautiful country.' Errors like this pose the very different problem of second language learning. What is more common is the kind of grammatical clumsiness or obscurity caused by a pupil handling complex ideas and perhaps over-extending himself syntactically. Indeed, a much neglected area in English teaching is textual cohesion, the way sentences are linked together and the way in which meaning is carried through a whole paragraph or series of paragraphs. There is some useful secondary school teaching to be done here, but again along the lines of 'How can you express yourself more effectively?'

Sometimes, of course, faulty grammar can lead to genuine ambiguity. A report on reading informs us that 'girls like reading more than boys'. Yet, in its context, this statement is not really ambiguous, and this is true of most of the ambiguities beloved by compilers of 'say what is unfortunately expressed in the following sentences' exercises. Many of these are either at the joke-book level: 'They are discussing fox-hunting in the House of Commons', 'Rocking-chair wanted for old gentleman with revolving bottom and wooden arms'; or are sentences which no one would actually utter:

'The boy was following the girl with a bicycle'; or are expressions which, even if not technically correct, everyone understands: 'It is always raining in Manchester.' If you are entering pupils for an examination which still sets this kind of exercise as a test of English, the long-term answer is to change your examination board. In the short term, instead of allowing the whole of the English curriculum to be distorted by the setting of artificial exercises, it is better to carry out special training exercises in the fourth and fifth year. Properly attacked, such exercises can be quite entertaining if ultimately rather futile.

Teaching grammatical nomenclature

It cannot be denied that there are many occasions on which it will be useful for teachers and pupils to use grammatical nomenclature. For instance, when reading a novel or poem the teacher may wish to draw attention to particular linguistic effects, and grammatical terms may be the most convenient way of doing this. 'What do you notice about the *verbs* in this passage?' 'Pick out the *adjectives* which create an impression of fear and terror.' Grammatical terminology can also be helpful when making other linguistic points: one may wish to discuss the use of commas to separate *subordinate clauses* from *main clauses*, or, in spelling, to talk about forming the *plurals* of nouns, or to point out that 'practice' is a *noun* and 'practise' a *verb*. Finally, in helping pupils improve the effectiveness of their own writing, grammatical terminology is often a useful shorthand. It is quite possible to talk about the use of 'joining words' and 'descriptive words', but there seems no good reason why, sooner or later, most secondary school pupils should not be introduced to technical terms like *conjunctions*, *adjectives* or *adverbs*; indeed, a familiarity with and general understanding of the commonest grammatical terms might be regarded as part of the general knowledge about their own language which secondary pupils ought to acquire.

However, this is not an argument for a fully-fledged course in formal grammar. Most of us have a general understanding of terms like 'sentence', 'noun', 'subject' without necessarily being able to define them precisely, or having experienced formal grammar teaching. (In fact, the precise grammatical definition of 'sentence' is one of the most controversial issues among linguists.) It is true that the most useful (perhaps the only) spin-off from traditional grammar teaching was to equip pupils with a number of technical terms which they could use for other purposes. But the superstructure of formal grammar teaching was quite unnecessary; we do not need to undertake elaborate exercises in parsing or clause analysis in order to be able to handle terms like subject, object, conjunction, noun, adverb. Very brief explanations (even, *pace* the linguists, incomplete explanations) will suffice to help pupils understand and use the terminology. Usually the explanation is best given as and when the need arises during the normal English programme – indeed, an understanding may often be implicitly developed simply by using the terms alongside the examples under consideration. The time to explain that 'adjectives describe nouns' may be when children are preparing to write a descriptive passage 'and when reading your descriptions I shall pay special attention to the adjectives you've used'. The fact that 'adjectives describe nouns' is a very incomplete, even grammatically unsound, definition is unimportant in this context, since to provide a functionally accurate and complete definition of 'adjective' would be time-wasting and too difficult for most 12-year-olds. Our aim is that pupils will gradually accumulate insights about the meaning and function of adjectives as the term 'adjective' is taught, from time to time, alongside an actual treatment of adjectives for some real purpose, so that the word, with its concept, becomes part of their vocabulary.

It is sometimes argued that, because teachers use grammatical terminology when helping pupils with their written work, grammar teaching has a part to play in helping pupils write more effectively. But this is to misunderstand the nature of the writing process. Grammatical terms may help to direct the pupil's attention to particular aspects of his writing, to isolate and hold in focus, say, different kinds of sentence structure or particular conjunctions. But actual improvement in writing comes about through practice, experimentation, variation, suiting form to purpose, and so on. The ability to connect sentences fluently in one's own writing is not helped by a course in clause analysis, though some knowledge of clauses and conjunctions may make it easier for teacher and pupils to discuss sentence structure. An apt analogy here is with spoken English. Our ability to speak fluently and effectively is not dependent on our objective knowledge of the intricacies of intonation, pitch, stress, (or, for that matter, the grammar of spoken English). But if we want to talk about and discuss spoken English we will find it useful to have some understanding of what is meant by 'intonation', 'pitch' and 'stress'.

Formal grammar teaching

A formal course in grammar teaching cannot, then, be justified either by attempts to teach 'correct' written English or by the desirability of pupils having some familiarity with grammatical nomenclature. The case for formal grammar teaching must rest on the intrinsic value of learning about the grammar of one's mother tongue. Since language is a central part of what it means to be human, and since language penetrates every moment of our waking lives, not just in communication with others but also in our innermost thoughts and feelings, then, it is argued, the study of language should be an essential part of education. Up to a point, one can readily concede this argument. It is to be hoped that most English teachers *will* possess a lively interest in language, not just language in use but language as an object of study.

Throughout the secondary school curriculum they will find and utilize many opportunities to put language 'under the microscope' for children to examine. But there are reasons why the grammatical system is perhaps the least suitable aspect of language for studying in this kind of way, compared with many other colourful and interesting aspects which might be examined.

In the first place, the analytic study of grammar is, as outlined in Chapter 1, a particularly abstract and difficult activity. Since it cannot be justified instrumentally, its intrinsic worth must depend on the enthusiasm and interest which can be generated among pupils. It might, indeed, be a suitable study for sixth forms, or for the more able pupils in the upper forms of secondary schools. One suspects that adults who remember with nostalgia their own grammar lessons ('I really enjoyed clause analysis') are in the main those adults who also got on rather well with Latin, Euclidean geometry and other equally esoteric pursuits.

There is a further daunting obstacle which faces any would-be grammar teacher – which grammar should he teach? Until about 1955 there was no problem. Grammar teaching was based on the traditional grammar handed down and perpetuated by school text-books for many decades, largely modelled on the grammar of Latin. Increasingly in the 1950s and 1960s this grammar became thoroughly discredited. English is *not* Latin, and the grammar of one language cannot be forced to fit the mould of another. Quite different categories of grammatical description are needed in English. For instance, whereas Latin is an inflected language, English relies mainly on word order to convey grammatical meaning; the subjunctive mood is hardly worth discussing in English; adverb clauses of purpose are about as omnipresent as the dodo in actual English usage. Since the grammar did not conform to actual English usage, it was necessary to invent language specimens, and a curious kind of grammar-exercise English grew up:

Hoping that he had not been seen, although he feared that the master had had a *too* watchful eye on him for some time, the boy who was determined to play truant on the day when the school was to be *addressed* by the local Member of Parliament slipped quietly through the door when the Head Prefect was called away and the door left unguarded. (From an 'O' level paper in which candidates were invited not only to analyse the 'sentence' into clauses, but also to name the part of speech and function of the three italicized words.)

Frequently, grammatical definitions combined form, function and meaning in a thoroughly unscientific way. Playing the grammar game meant becoming adept in a self-contained world, with its own data and rules, which bore little relation to the real language world. Because of this, grammar teaching was mainly prescriptive and deductive – pupils were told what the rules were, and then had to apply them to carefully selected material.

But if traditional grammar is dead, what is to replace it? Here the teacher is faced by a bewildering multiplicity of choices. There is widespread agreement that grammars should be descriptive, that categories and structures should be arrived at pragmatically by an analysis of actual language data. Even here, however, transformational grammarians argue that we need to penetrate beyond the surface features of language to arrive at 'deep' structure, and this means taking into account native speakers' intuitive understanding of the underlying meaning. Apart from this broad agreement on method, there is little consensus about systems, categories or terminology. The teacher faces the problem of choosing among many competing grammars, with no simple, widely accepted grammar for school use. Moreover, the grammatical scene is constantly changing – today's orthodoxy may be tomorrow's heresy – and many of the systems have a formidable jargon and complex methodology.

Does this mean that *no* viable grammar teaching can be undertaken in schools? If one starts with the assumption that there are no clear-cut answers, but that language *does* have a grammatical system and that this system can, in principle, be discovered, then some interesting inductive grammatical study can be initiated. The aim of such study is not primarily to discover linguistic facts, but to experience what it is like to be a linguist – what grammatical enquiry means. The linguist makes hypotheses about the grammar, then tests his hypotheses against the linguistic data, and confirms or modifies his original theories. There is no reason why pupils cannot be exposed to (selected/monitored) samples of language, given help with analytic methods, and encouraged to develop and test hypotheses about how grammar works. Language is very suitable for this kind of controlled induction which in many ways parallels inductive methods in scientific enquiry.

Some examples of this kind of work will be given in Chapter 7. However, many English teachers may not be equipped by their training to initiate grammatical enquiry; indeed, the background and interests of some teachers may prejudice them against it. Unless they have done some relevant linguistics as part of their degree, they are unlikely to have the knowledge or confidence needed to handle the free-ranging enquiry and critical questioning which will arise. There is, therefore, a very real danger that linguistically naive teachers may fall back on prescriptive and unscientific kinds of grammar teaching. It is worth stressing again that formal grammar teaching has no direct utility, and that grammatical enquiry is best regarded as an 'optional extra' for older pupils. To tackle it successfully, a teacher needs to be both enthusiastic himself and able to inspire interest in his pupils. If in doubt, miss it out.

References

1. The development of grammar in the writing of junior school children is outlined in W. Harpin, *The Second 'R'* (Allen & Unwin, 1976).

2. *Language Performance in Schools*: Secondary Survey Report No. 1 (HMSO, 1982) Par. 4. 134, p. 100.

3. C. Barber, *Linguistic Change in Present-day English* (Oliver & Boyd, 1964), p. 8. He accuses Fowler of quoting examples of actual usage and then saying what they 'ought' to have been.

PART TWO
PRACTICAL MATTERS

5

WAYS OF
IMPROVING SPELLING

I AN INDIVIDUAL SPELLING PROGRAMME

Any effective teaching of spelling in the secondary school must be based on individual learning. A pupil needs to practise those words which he himself spells incorrectly, his personal 'spelling demons', not words which his classmates spell wrongly, nor words which his teacher decides he 'ought' to learn. Given the wide range of individual spelling needs in a secondary school classroom, to set the same spelling exercises to the whole class, or routinely to follow some course-book or graded spelling scheme, will usually be both inefficient and ineffective. If, on the other hand, a pupil has the evidence of improved spelling in his own written work, he will have the motivation to persevere with regular spelling practice and the confidence to believe that he can succeed. Therefore, a systematic and well organized programme of individualized spelling instruction lies at the heart of any successful attempt to improve children's spelling.

Such a programme will have the following basic elements:

1 A personal spelling book, in which the pupil records those words whose spelling he is currently attempting to master.

2 A personal dictionary into which he transfers words when their spelling has been mastered.

3 A system of spelling workcards to which pupils can be referred for the reinforcement of particular points of spelling. These workcards may be supported by worksheets to provide practice exercises.

4 An arrangement for the regular testing of spelling which will not occupy unreasonable amounts of class or teacher time. It is probably best if children work in pairs, testing each other from the spelling books. No more than five minutes need be given over to this, say, twice a week.

The personal spelling book

Each child should have his own spelling book (this is more satisfactory than using the back of his English exercise book) ruled to provide:

(*a*) space for the word being learned,

(*b*) space for hints on how the word may be remembered (a line or two under the word is best),

(*c*) dated columns to indicate successful or unsuccessful testings of the word.

A typical page in a spelling book might look like the figure opposite.

Note that, where appropriate, the words are clearly set out in syllables and the 'trouble spots' highlighted by underlining, capitalizing, or, perhaps most effectively, by the use of coloured crayon or pen. Ticks and crosses indicate successful and unsuccessful testings, D that the word has been transferred to the personal dictionary (having been spelt successfully in six tests spread over three weeks), T that the teacher's help has been sought, and W that a workcard has been used. It is

Word	Entered	17.9	21.9	24.9	28.9	1.10	5.10	8.10	12.10	15.10
re-sid-Ent someone who resides	14.9	X	✓	X	✓	✓	✓	✓	✓	✓D
sIEge i before e, except after c	14.9	✓	✓	✓	✓	✓	✓D			
sight you need good sight for night flight	17.9		✓	✓	✓	✓	✓	✓D		
Feb-Ru-ar-y February BRings the Rain	17.9		X	X	✓	✓	✓	✓	✓	✓D
sta-tion say stat-i-on	21.9			X	X	✓	X	X	X T W	✓
PIG-eon picture the flying PIG	24.9				X	✓	✓	✓	✓	✓

important that not too many words are currently being held in the spelling book (a maximum might be twenty), and that the teacher occasionally looks at a pupil's spelling book and personal dictionary and, perhaps, administers a short test himself.

Another way of organizing the spelling programme is for each pupil to build up a collection of personal spelling cards, retained in a box file. This is a more expensive system, but is more flexible and easier to use. There is more space on the cards for display and for *aides-mémoire*, they are easier to handle for practice and testing, and when a word has been learned its card may be withdrawn, the withdrawn cards forming an adjustable personal dictionary. The use of spelling cards is especially advocated with older pupils and good spellers.

Marking spelling errors

Words to be entered in the spelling book may come from many sources. A pupil may enter words which he comes across in his reading or which the teacher suggests should be learned. When proof-reading his own written work he may find words of whose spelling he is unsure and which he needs to look up in a dictionary. However, the most important source is likely to be errors which the teacher finds in his written work and draws to his attention. Since traditional 'spelling corrections' are largely a waste of time (little is learned by just copying out correct spellings), I suggest the teacher uses a symbol (SP) to indicate a word which he wants the pupil to enter in his spelling book and learn. In deciding which words so to mark, the teacher might bear in mind the following points:

1.   The most important comments on a pupil's work are those which indicate how the teacher has responded to it, and which bear on its content, effectiveness and interest. Except, therefore, for the occasional exercise which the teacher may set to give practice in technical skills, comments on spelling should always be unobtrusive. 'Watch your spelling!!!' may be therapeutic for the teacher but achieves little for the pupil.

2.   Don't splatter the pupils' work with red ink or other marks. Nothing is better calculated to put a child off writing than to be continually pulled up for technical errors. Probably three or four spelling errors per piece of work are all that should be marked for learning. A teacher who marks every technical error is simply demonstrating his own skill at proof-reading.

3.   It follows that errors marked by the teacher should be related to a pupil's spelling competence. If a pupil is making numerous elementary errors, it is pointless asking him to learn difficult and unusual words; the teacher must pick out those errors which he feels are basic and important. A major criterion will be their usefulness to the pupil – are these words which he will need to spell over and over again? Conversely, if a pupil is normally a good speller, one can ask him to learn more difficult words.

4.   Usually the teacher will want to write out the correct spelling, indicating clearly that part of the word causing difficulty and perhaps suggesting a way in which the spelling

might be remembered.

5.   Pupils will have their individual spelling weaknesses, and certain types of spelling error will tend to repeat themselves (for instance, uncertainty about vowel combinations, doubled letters, or consonant groups). When a teacher spots such a weakness, he can direct the pupil to the appropriate workcard and worksheet. This can easily be done if the workcards are coded, and the code written alongside the word.

6.   Genuine misspellings should not be confused with slips of the pen or with carelessness. If a piece of work is especially carelessly written, according to a pupil's normal standards, it is best not to mark it until he has proof-read it and submitted a revised draft.

7.   When marking, the teacher should have beside him a book for recording a brief note on each pupil's spelling performance, including words he has asked him to learn and perhaps other comments. This record will also serve to highlight errors which are being made by many pupils and which may warrant more general attention.

To illustrate these suggestions, a short essay is reproduced, with spellings marked, as follows:

Karen (age 12)

A busy market day

My father owns a stall on the market the stall sells potry, vases etc. He gets all the stuff from a factory which makes things like plates and anything to do with china.

SP   I sometimes help him on a Saturday because my
      freinds dad owns a fruit and veg stall on the market
*1   and she goes and help * him with it every Saturday.

. . .

My mother and brother like coming to market with us on a Saturday so we have a helper called Reg. Reg is
SP   in his early thirtees, he came to us looking for a job after his wife died. He recently got a good job but he

said he would still come and help us every Saturday and he kept his word.

. . .

*2   The sad thing is packing up time on Market day, if my dad has done well then he is * a good mood but if
SP   we haven't done well then he is <u>dissapointed</u>.

fr I E nd
(a friend <u>in</u> <u>nee</u>d
is a friend <u>ind</u><u>ee</u>d)

thirty – thirties
PLUR . 3

dis – appoin^ted
PREF . 1

Notes
Sp indicates that a word is to be entered in the personal spelling book and learned.

PLURAL 3 and PREFIX 1 direct Karen to the appropriate workcards for further practice. The teacher would need to feel that these errors were not just isolated cases before doing this.

In 'friend' the trouble spot is emphasized and a way of remembering it suggested.

*1 and *2 look like slips of the pen. Karen had not had a chance to proof-read her essay before handing it in.

Not every spelling mistake needs to be marked. In line 2 'potry' has not been picked up. For the marking of a child with more severe spelling problems than Karen, see p. 56.

Of course, the main comment should be on the content of the essay — a chatty, personal account, but not really re-creating the noise and bustle of market day, which was the point of the exercise. One might want to talk to Karen about this. One also notes that she might well talk to the rest of the class about her own experiences of working on a market stall.

Strategies for learning spelling

If children are left to their own devices when trying to learn spellings, they are likely to use inefficient learning techniques which will quickly lead to failure and loss of motivation. Perhaps the single most useful service which teachers can offer children to help them improve their spelling is to show them *how* to go about learning spellings for themselves. It is worthwhile spending some time teaching efficient learning techniques to children when they first enter secondary school, and periodically reinforcing these techniques until they become second nature.

Briefly, in order that a word whose spelling is not yet mastered should become spelt correctly as a matter of habit, three things are necessary:

1 The word must be correctly perceived in the first place. (The child must *see* it and *hear* it correctly.)
2 The image of the word must be retained in some form after its removal. (The retention may be visual, auditory, kinaesthetic or any combination of these – most experts recommend a 'multi-sensory' approach.)
3 The correct motor habit must be formed through practice in writing the word.

The first stage in helping a child to learn to spell, therefore, is to get him to study the word carefully. He should look at it and pronounce it. He should break it down into syllables and look at and pronounce each of these separately. He should notice any 'hard spots', for instance parts that are not spelt as they are pronounced, and should emphasize these in some way. He could mark the hard spot with red ink, or say it out loud while whispering the rest of the word.

The second stage is to retain the image of the word. The child should cover the word up or turn it over and try to write it from memory.

(*a*) He may try to visualize the word, both as a whole and in its constituent parts, focusing on the hard spot.

(*b*) He may try to say the word to himself, both the whole word and its constituent parts, emphasizing the hard spot.

(*c*) Some poor spellers may be helped by the technique of 'finger-tracing', whereby the word is written clearly and boldly and the child then traces the outline of the letters with his finger. If children get used to this technique early in their secondary school career, there is no reason why it need prove embarrassing later on.

(*d*) He may use one of a variety of mnemonics to help him remember the word. The teacher may suggest an appropriate mnemonic, but the pupils should be encouraged to develop the habit of inventing their own mnemonics.

Children should be introduced to these different techniques for learning spelling and develop the method or combination of methods which suits them best.

The third stage is for the spelling to become automatic. *Short* periods of practice, frequently repeated, are much more effective than long sessions spent poring over spelling books. Children should get into the habit of filling in the odd spare moments in school, or spending five minutes each night, practising their spellings. They should first try to write the words *without* reference to their spelling books, and then check their efforts. It is important to attempt active recall, since simply copying the word out is of little benefit. The pay-off comes when the child correctly spells the word without thinking in his own written work.

To summarize, on their entry to secondary school, children need training in the use of their personal spelling books and careful guidance with techniques of learning spelling. At first, the teacher can regularly allow ten minutes at the end of some lessons for the pupils to work in pairs: five minutes for learning their spellings and five minutes for testing each other. The teacher will also need to check from time to time that spelling books are being maintained and that spelling practice is being kept up – the children will take learning to spell seriously only if the teacher does. It is worth spending time in the early weeks to ensure that regular routines are established. One teacher urged on pupils the slogan: 'CLASS 1W ARE WOW' (Class 1W agreed rules ensure wonderful original writing), while another provided his pupils with an outline of the steps to be followed, to be kept in the front of their spelling books.

LEARN HOW TO SPELL
or how to beat your spelling demons in three
easy stages.

A. LOOK at the word carefully.
SAY the word aloud.
SPLIT the word into its parts.
NOTICE any hard spots. (Why is it a demon?)

B. Cover the word up and try to write it from memory. To help you remember you can –
PICTURE the word to yourself. Can you see each part in turn? Can you see the tricky part?
SAY the word to yourself. Can you say each part? Can you say the tricky part?
TRACE the word with your finger, saying it as you trace it.
INVENT a way of remembering the tricky part.

C. Now write the word in your spelling book so as to bring out the tricky part, and underneath write a way of remembering the word. Use colour and drawings if you want to.

EVERY DAY find time to practise the words in your spelling book for a few minutes.

Write the word down without looking at your book. Then check –
Have you got it right?
Notice the parts you get wrong
and try again.

REMEMBER:
A practice a day,
Keeps the demons at bay.

Children with special spelling problems

As we saw in Chapter 2, there are many reasons why words may be spelt wrongly, and why individual children may have special problems with spelling. If children acquire good habits for learning spelling and if the teacher acquaints them with a variety of techniques for memorizing words, then most of them will find out which strategies suit them best. However, there are two major causes of poor spelling for which the teacher may be able to suggest those approaches likely to be most fruitful.

It is assumed that, apart from children who have great difficulty reading, and who need special remedial help, visual and auditory discrimination will not be a major problem for secondary school children. The two likeliest causes of chronically poor spelling at the secondary stage are poor visual memory and poor auditory memory. The types of spelling error children with these weaknesses produce are illustrated in the two essays which follow, both written by children judged not to need remedial help with reading.

Andrew (age 12)

A busy Railway Station

A busy day in a railway station engines starting of, making a big nouse brakes squelling Gardes shouting "All doors cloosed," "hung on now madom" on
SP comes the ladey on the speker "Will pasengers going to London please go to platform 2, thank you" people shoving to get to there train, Kides runing every were, the cafe and snake que getting biger, people trying to
SP leve and people pushing back so they can get in, mini cars taking lugeg people stoping them and asking "Where's platform 2". On comes the speker again "whille all pasengers enbarking to Nottingham please go to platform 8 thank you".

squEAling }
spEAker } EA
lEAve   }

ruNNing }
biGGer   } SUFF. 2
stoPPing }

Andrew exemplifies much the most common cause of poor spelling by children who are competent readers – poor visual recall. The writing is characterized by spellings which are for the most part 'phonetic' – 'good' guesses based on what a word sounds like. But Andrew cannot picture what a word should look like. Traditional methods of teaching spelling, which involve 'staring' at words, are of no help to Andrew. He should be encouraged to use auditory methods, pronouncing the word carefully, syllable by syllable. This should be supported by workcards helping him to construct phonically the many regular sound–symbol correspondences that underlie English spelling. He also needs to develop a range of strategies for remembering particular words, and it is possible that finger-tracing may prove an effective aid.

The most important thing in marking Andrew's work is to comment on his very considerable success in capturing the noise and bustle of a busy railway station. (There is even a certain breathlessness created by his failure to paragraph speech properly!) Andrew *knows* he is a bad speller – there is no point in covering the essay with SP marks or worrying about spellings like 'lugege' or 'enbarking'. Instead, six words have been underlined (four to be entered in the spelling book and learned) illustrating two common errors, and Andrew sent to workcards to practise the regular phonic sequences involved.

Rebecca (age 12)

<u>A Busy Market Day</u>

As I walk onto the market I can hear the sound of the fish men and the fuirt sellers chatting they small verse.

Than we came to the shoes store and the mertral store the sound of shoes is rather quite people taking all the time saying all the diffent vesrsers.

Sometimes I meet a frinerd and we start to talk abot diffent things. Than as we talk it strats to rain it prous it down people put umbrlles up and plastic gose over the stalls to keep every thing dry.

Rebecca clearly has auditory problems. She cannot put together the constituent sounds of a word, and so makes random guesses. She has problems over sequencing (fuirt, prous, strats), and syllabizing (diffent, frinerd). Her errors tend not to be phonetic since she cannot hear in her mind what a word sounds like (mertral, vesrsers). Normal methods of phonic instruction are unlikely to help Rebecca. She should be encouraged to visualize words, either whole words or syllable by syllable rather than by individual letters. Finger-tracing may be helpful, and repeated attempts to write the word swiftly will reinforce learning the longer units of word and syllable. Since her reading is competent, she should be encouraged to read her own work aloud, looking carefully at what she has written and pronouncing it as it stands. Neither Andrew nor Rebecca has experienced a systematic spelling programme at secondary school, and while spelling may remain a problem for them, there is no reason why they cannot be given the confidence to believe they *can* improve.

Memory aids for spelling

It has been stressed so far in this chapter that pupils may be helped to master their own particular 'spelling demons' by *aides-mémoire* of various kinds. Most adults will have their own battery of devices, well-known (stalaCtites Come from the Ceiling, stalaGmites Grow from the Ground) or idiosyncratic (the principal is a real PAL). Children, too, will delight in using these tricks and may well invent their own, but the teacher will often want to make suggestions from the following list:

Spelling rules. These are discussed later, but the general principles are that the pupil *needs* the rule (i.e. he is making frequent mistakes and not just getting one word wrong), and that it should be easy to understand and apply.

Word structure. Pupils should learn how to break words into syllables and other constituent parts. Examining prefixes and suffixes, revealing words hidden in other words, may all give a clue to the spelling: sincere-ly, dis-appear, mis-spell, is-land, senTENced (for ten years!)

Association with related words: resident—reside, separate—part, condemn—condemnation.

Association by similarity. There is an important principle here: treating together words of similar sound but different spelling only causes confusion; words should be associated with similarly spelt words, to establish spelling regularities. So, 'here' and 'hear' should not be taught together; instead associate 'here, there, where' to establish a meaning/spelling link, 'hear, ear, rear, fear, near' to establish a sound/spelling link. Often the association can be established by a (silly) sentence:

The peng*ui*n spilt fr*ui*t j*ui*ce down his new s*ui*t.

Good s*ight* needed for n*ight* fl*ight*.

H*ere*, th*ere* and everywh*ere*.

Association by contrast. As just discussed, this can cause confusion and should be advocated only when one word of a pair is firmly fixed. For instance, if a current of water or electricity is thoroughly mastered, then 'currant' cake can be remembered as being different; if you are quite sure that the principal is a pal, then you may also remember that he isn't a man of principle.

Association by meaning or context: 'sincerely, faithfully, truly' might be remembered as a group arising from letter writing.

'Spelling' pronunciations. This is a method of wide general applicability, especially for pupils with poor visual recall. Probably the children say 'wensdi'; pronounce it 'Wed-nes-day'. Try saying 'sep-Ar-ate', with a long ā sound as in 'part'. Use the American pronunciation of 'harássment' with the stress on the second syllable (provided you remember to pronounce it properly in class!) Roll the 'r' in 'Febrrruary'. A

great many words can be remembered in this way, however bizarre the pronunciation.

Derivation and origin. This is a particularly useful method when links can be made with languages the pupils are learning, especially where the foreign pronunciation gives a clue to the English spelling: environment (French: environ), supersede (Latin: super-sedere – to sit over or above), Latin 'scire' (to know) producing science, conscience, etc.

Rhymes, jingles and other mnemonics: You *hear* with your *ear*. The 'c' must be seen in 'scene'. Stationery includes *en*velopes; station*ary* st*a*nds still. In February we say "BRR".

Visual associations. This can be a very powerful technique, especially if a bizarre visual image can be formed. You are unlikely to forget 'pigeon' if it calls to mind a bird with snout and curly tail. Children can be encouraged to make their own idiosyncratic connections and share them with the class. One adult remembers 'bachelor' by visualizing the Kings' Singers in concert – a group of bachelors singing Bach.

Proof-reading

Another important habit for children to acquire is that of proof-reading their work before handing it in. The teacher should emphasize that a carelessly written piece of work is discourteous to the reader, and should return the work where it is obvious that a pupil has not taken the trouble to at least check through for blatant errors. Proof-reading, however, is a skill that has to be learned, and there are a number of ways in which teachers can help with this.

1.   Let the children see that you redraft your work. Write alongside them sometimes and discuss re-drafting with them. Of course, proof-reading is only a small part of the re-drafting process. You will want to discuss with them a whole range of 'improvements' that can be made to written work, including pre-eminently matters of content and expression – how can we make the piece of writing more effective and fitted to its

purpose? Nevertheless, correcting spelling is a part of this, and it will add greatly to the force of the argument if pupils see that *you* sometimes spell a word wrongly, or are unsure of a spelling and have recourse to a dictionary.

2. Introduce the pupils to some signs which they can use when proof-reading, rings, arrows, ∧ , ℧ , and the like. A useful exercise is for them to re-draft a piece of work written by someone else – perhaps another child of about their age – either individually or as part of a group or class joint exercise. Occasionally it might be worthwhile setting an exercise where the aim is just to polish up technical points.

A third-year, top band class had been given the task of writing a story containing a number of unusual objects. To illustrate the need for re-drafting, the teacher wrote on the board a passage from a pupil's story which had been read to the class and praised. The class discussed the changes needed, and indicated them with proof-reading annotations.

He pushed the door of Proffesor Williams study open. Inside the room was in a right state. The Proffesor was laying accross his desk with the remains of a half eaten cheese sandwich in front of him. His right hand had been flung out knocking a blue glass paperweight onto the floor. In his hand he had a green plant with purple flowers. Holmes looked round the scene. 'Now Watson what would you diagnose.'

The class used ◯ to indicate a spelling mistake and ∿ to suggest an improvement to the style. ('Held' or 'clutched' were offered instead of 'had' and 'surveyed' instead of 'looked round'.)

3. Although pupils should not have to interrupt the flow of creative writing to worry about spelling, it is good practice for them to indicate in some way that they are unsure of a word's spelling, for example 'confidance', 'conf.(?)'. This greatly assists proof-reading.

4. Proof-reading for spelling needs to be taught, since

ordinary 'scanning' reading is not sufficient. (If they don't believe this, slip a few spelling errors into a passage, without telling them, and see how many they spot.) Close examination of every detail is necessary, so stress that they look at each word in isolation and that they scrutinize each word carefully, reading rigorously from left to right. The technique can easily be illustrated using blackboard or overhead projector. Reading one's work aloud will often show up careless errors.

5.   Proof-reading is best done 'cold', so try to have a gap between the original writing and the later checking. There is no harm in getting someone else to check your work, so that it is an activity that can be done in pairs, or at home.

HOW TO CHECK SPELLINGS

An important part of proof-reading is to know what to do when one is uncertain how to spell a word. Children should be made aware of a range of strategies which may be used.

(a) Write down alternative spellings of the word. Which one 'looks' right?

(b) Pronounce a doubtful word. Does it 'sound' right?

(c) Can you break the word down into syllables and spell syllable by syllable? Look at each syllable and say each syllable.

(d) Do you know any rule or other aid which can help you?

(e) Does the origin of the word suggest the likely spelling? Can you think of any other words associated with or related to this one?

(f) Look it up in a dictionary.

(g) If all else fails ask someone else.

DICTIONARIES

In connection with (f) above, dictionary skills need to be taught. This can be done quite quickly, and a lot of time need not be spent on elaborate dictionary-hunting exercises. As far as spelling is concerned the following dictionary skills are essential: an understanding of alphabetical order (including more than just the first letter: for instance, how strong, straw, strain, strap, stave, and St Vitus' dance would be arranged), familiarity with the lay-out of dictionaries (including the use of guide-words), how to look up words derived by adding prefixes, suffixes, or by stem change (e.g. strength, told). Different dictionaries may do this in slightly different ways, and spelling dictionaries are available in which derived words are clearly listed after their stem words. Other dictionary skills which bear some relation to spelling are being able to interpret pronunciation and stress from a dictionary, and looking up the origins of words. But the dictionary should be regarded as a useful tool and will not normally be the main focus of attention in an English lesson.

It goes without saying that each pupil should have access to a dictionary, preferably his own copy, but it is important not to over-use the dictionary during the original writing, so that the flow keeps being interrupted. Instead, mark the doubtful word in some way and check it later. Dictionaries should be used to look up words which a pupil has already attempted to spell.

Spelling workcards and worksheets

We have suggested that an effective system of individual spelling needs to be supported by workcards and worksheets, so that where a teacher detects a particular spelling weakness he may direct the pupil to the appropriate workcards and worksheets. Commercially produced workcards are available, but while a carefully graded and systematic workcard scheme may be useful in the early stages of learning spelling, or with remedial groups, it needs using judiciously in the normal secondary classroom, with the teacher prepared to modify and add to the scheme. He will find some of the material too simple, or inappropriate in other ways, and most schemes use a concept of graded spelling competence (even 'spelling-age') which is of dubious validity with secondary school pupils. An English department probably does best to build up its own stock of spelling cards suited to the needs of its own classes. This will take time in the early stages, but will provide an invaluable resource in due course.

Workcards may profitably be of three kinds.

WORKCARDS FOR SPELLING RULES

There are many 'rules' which may be reinforced by using workcards. The general principle is to group together on one card useful or common words which illustrate *one aspect* of the rule, together with an explanation of the rule. An accompanying worksheet provides practice exercises and other tasks. (These worksheets might be regarded as optional. There is a danger of children wasting time on boring and artificial exercises. A child should practise only words which he genuinely has trouble with and then only for short periods of time – say fifteen minutes at the most.)

Useful spelling rules are discussed later, but we may take a series of workcards on the formation of plurals as an example.

Plural card 1
Most words form their plural by adding -s. (The -s emphasized in some way, probably by colour.) This is followed by a list of ten or so common words of the type dog – dogs, again with the 's' emphasized.
Note: It is very unlikely you would need to use this particular card, since few non-remedial secondary pupils will be having problems with straightforward plurals; it is included here for completeness.

Plural card 2

This is shown in full, together with some examples of the kind of question one might include on a worksheet, as follows.

Plural 2			
If a word ends in -s, -x, -sh, -ch, add -ES to make the plural.			
circus	circuses	dish	dishes
bus	buses	brush	brushes
fox	foxes	watch	watches
box	boxes	branch	branches
Can you work out why we add ES and not just S?			

Plural 2 Worksheet

1. Read the workcard carefully, then cover it up. We add -ES to a word to make the plural if the word ends with _____, _____, _____, _____ (4 endings).

2. Can you answer the question on the workcard? Say each word to yourself. What would happen if we tried to add just -s? Say it to yourself.

3. Write out the following story, putting in the right plural form.

As the (clock) and (watch) in the (house) showed midnight, a sudden gust of wind shook the (branch) of the (tree). A family of (fox) crept through the (bush), their (nose) scenting the air, their (brush) tense. The (fox) scarcely disturbed the (flower) and long (grass) under their (paw). Suddenly, two loud (crash) shattered the silence of the night.

Check your answers with the back of the workcard.

4. Make a list of 12 other words (nouns); 3 each ending in -s, -x, -ch and -sh. Write down their plurals and use each plural in a sentence.

5. Start at the letter S in the middle of this word square and find 8 plural words by moving one square up, down, sideways

or diagonally in any direction. The 8 words are

A – – –   B – – – – – –
C – – – – – – –   D – – – – –
F – – – –   R – – – – – –
S – – – –   W – – – – – –

How many of the words have added ES to make the plural?
(Be careful).

S	F	E	S	R	W	I
E	O	X	R	A	S	T
H	B	A	T	H	C	S
I	S	B	Ⓢ	S	E	E
T	A	U	R	B	H	S
S	X	C	C	U	S	I
E	S	I	R	E	S	D

Plural card 3
Words ending in -y. The teacher could here make use of the
'disappearing y', for instance:
    baby   bab*   babi   babies
since this rule also applies to -y before other suffixes:
    happier, marriage, carried.
    In general, a teacher with artistic talent will have plenty of
scope to exercise it when designing workcards!

Plural card 4
Words ending in vowel + y, e.g. day, donkey, toy, guy.

Plural cards 5 and 6
Words ending in -o which add -es and which add -s. The cards might well include tips on how to remember which was which, but a pupil would normally be directed to only *one* of these cards at any one time.

Plural card 7
Words ending in -f and -fe, e.g. half, knife.

Plural card 8
Exceptions to 7, e.g. roof, cliff. Note the general principle that exceptions to rules should be learned separately; indeed it may be better to learn them quite apart from a consideration of the rule.

Plural card 9
Irregular plurals, e.g. man, child, goose, foot. Again, this is a card which one might never use, since a child spelling, say, 'women' incorrectly is not necessarily having problems with irregular plurals in general.

Plural card 10
Zero plurals, e.g. sheep, deer, fish. One might make this a 'ragbag' card and also include oddities like 'scissors', 'trousers'.

Plural card 11
Foreign plurals, e.g. formula, cherub, locus. Since this card will only be given to good spellers, it would be an interesting worksheet exercise to ask them to hunt up the origins of these words and hence the reasons for their spelling. One might also ask them to distinguish pairs such as indexes/indices, appendixes/appendices, brothers/brethren, pennies/pence.

Plural card 12
Compound plurals, e.g. mothers-in-law, will-o'-the-wisps.

Other spelling rules may be dealt with similarly. Remember:

(*a*) One card should deal with one aspect of the rule only.

(*b*) Keep exceptions separate from rule-following words.

(*c*) Use visual devices to highlight the rule.

(*d*) Where possible, give tips for remembering the rule.

(*e*) The particular word which the child has spelt wrongly will have been entered in his spelling book and practised in the usual way. So don't send him to the workcard unless he needs to understand the rule and don't ask him to do the worksheet unless he really needs to practise the rule.

(*f*) Make the worksheet exercises as interesting as you can (see the later suggestions for class exercises).

WORKCARDS FOR WORD-BUILDING

These are useful when a pupil is having difficulty with prefixes and suffixes, or with breaking words down into constituent syllables. Particular trouble spots may be suffixes like -er/-or, -able/-ible, -ly/-ally, -ent/-ant or the correct form of prefixes (in– im– il– ir–). As before, each workcard should deal with one point at a time (keep 'eatable' away from 'edible', and don't let your 'sailor' near your 'farmer'), use words which will be useful to the children, and make the visual layout as clear as poss-Ible.

WORKCARDS FOR REGULAR TROUBLE SPOTS

The most frequent use of workcards will be to present words which share a common difficulty. The card should, by its design, highlight the 'trouble spot' and offer some advice on how to remember it. Some of the more common trouble spots are:

Unusual or difficult consonant combinations: silent letters (b, g, k, p), combinations with h (ch, tch, sch, gh, ph, rh, wh), combinations with u (gu, qu, squ), sc and wr. Below is a specimen workcard for 'wh'.

WH	
	when where why what
	who whether while which
	whale whip wheat
	Sound the H as you say the word.
	WHisper the word – can you hear it WHistle?

Note: This workcard illustrates the important principle of treating similar words together. 'Where' and 'whether' are dealt with here so that they can be associated with similar words and kept apart from 'weather', 'were' and 'we're'.

Difficult vowel combinations. You will probably need workcards for many of the standard long vowel graphemes including:

day	nail	whale
bear	pair	share
calm	farm	
fear	peer	tier
bean	keen	
home	toast	toe
blue	flew	room
down	shout	
floor	yawn	

Difficult final syllables. The trickiest of these is the -ough grapheme with its many pronunciations. Others are -igh, -ight, -ought, -aught, -cede, -ceed, -tion.

Other trouble spots, for instance:

(i) Words with single doubled consonants, e.g. across, harass, necessary, occur, recommend, professor, succeed.

(*ii*)   Words with double doubled consonants, e.g. accommodate, address, committee, embarrass, possess.

(*iii*) Words where letters are often added, e.g. light(e)ning, ath(e)lete, burg(u)lar, bu(i)siness, long(t)itude, monst(e)rous/disast(e)rous, mischiev(i)ous, umb(e)rella.

(*iv*)   Words where letters are often missed out, e.g. diff(e)rent, Feb(r)uary, prob(ab)ly.

(*v*)   Words where the spelling varies according to the part of speech – practice/practise, etc.

It is possible to list a great many words whose spelling causes problems, but there is little point in this. Every teacher will discover the spelling demons which his own classes have, and devise workcards accordingly. The workcards should be coded for easy reference and filed with the code visible. A simple code is sufficient: 'ie/ei 3', for instance, would direct a pupil to the third card dealing with the 'i before e' rule, or '-ll-' to a card dealing with doubled 'l' in the middle of words. However, it is important to reiterate that workcards should not be over-used – indeed, as their use diminishes, so a teacher knows that his spelling policy is succeeding (or, at least, that his pupils' spelling is improving!). Pupils should regard them not as a dull, repetitive treadmill, but as an occasional tool which they discover helps them to master words they were not able to spell previously.

II   CLASS INSTRUCTION IN SPELLING

So far this chapter has stressed the importance of individual learning as the basis of spelling instruction. To repeat— frequent and lengthy class instruction is ineffective, because it tends to be insensitive to individual problems, and inefficient, because it detracts from more useful ways of spending the time. Particularly to be deplored are the traditional dictation exercises to the whole class and the setting of artificial exercises of the 'filling in the gap' or other equally futile varieties. This is not to say that teachers should *never* raise spelling points with or set exercises for the whole class, or organize spelling games or activities. But before he embarks on class instruction, a teacher should feel reasonably confident that a sufficiently large number of pupils are going to benefit from it to make the exercise worthwhile.

Spelling rules

When a teacher finds that a number of pupils are having similar spelling difficulties which are covered by one of the so-called spelling 'rules', he may feel it is worthwhile spending class time considering the rule. Most spelling rules in English have numerous sub-rules and exceptions, so that they are best regarded as 'rules of thumb' rather than strict dicta. The following rules are those which have sufficient generality to be worth considering dealing with in class.

1. i before e except after c, when the sound is -ee- as in 'feet'. (Exceptions: seize, weird, weir, counterfeit, protein, plebeian. Note, too, that the rule does not apply to words like height, rein, friend, where the vowel sound is not -ee-.)

2. The disappearing y. y→i before suffixes: beautiful, happily, carried, various, marriage (exceptions: shyly, slyly, piteous); sub-rules: (*a*) vowel + y keeps the y — enjoyment, boyish, journeying (exceptions: said, paid, laid, daily); (*b*) consonant + y keeps the y before -ing; tidying, trying (and note tying, dying).

3. Magic e.
e added to a one-syllable word makes the vowel sound long: hop/hope, mad/made, shin/shine. (Exception: sing/singe — what difference does the 'e' make here?)

4. Rules for adding suffixes to one-syllable words:
   (*a*) if the suffix begins with a vowel, a final consonant is doubled: hopping, shinning, sadder,
   (*b*) but a final -e is dropped: hoping, shining, famous

(exceptions: singeing, dyeing – why is the 'e' retained?),

(*c*) the word is unchanged if the suffix begins with a consonant: sadly, tamely, careful (exceptions: awful, duly, truly, wholly, ninth).

5. Rules for adding suffixes to longer words.

(*a*) Final -e is dropped before a vowel but kept before a consonant (this is an extension of 4 above): advisory, providing, debatable, sincerely, appeasement (exceptions: noticeable – why?, argument, and alternatives such as judgement/judgment).

(*b*) The rule when to double a final consonant before a vowel was given in Chapter 2. It is a complex one but may be remembered by

> If stressed you double,
> Not stressed don't trouble

and 'fixed' by critical pairs such as preférred/préference, reférred/súffered (exceptions: -l usually doubles regardless of stress – travelled, marvellous, but note paralleled and parallelogram, and most -ity endings – mentality, equality.)

6. Leave the word unaltered when adding a prefix:

dis-appear   mis-take
dis-solve   mis-spell

7. -ll- usually becomes -l- when added to another word: always, already, altogether, hopeful, skilful, until.

TEACHING SPELLING RULES

The above are, perhaps, the most common rules on which the teacher may wish to spend class time, though there are many other patterns and regularities which he may want to draw attention to from time to time. *How* to teach the rules is another matter, since prescriptive teaching of rules may be confusing for many children. One of the most effective techniques is to allow the children to work out the rules for themselves, inductively. (If it is objected that the children are not 'clever' enough to do this, then almost certainly they are not going to be able to understand the rule when it is pronounced ex cathedra by the teacher.)

The following lesson plan might be appropriate for a second or third year class.

1. Divide the class into groups of, say, five or six.
2. Each group is given a list of words (or the teacher may write them on the board), for instance: reach, poacher, marching, catch, witch, choose, chips, watching.
3. They are set the problem to solve as a group. 'You are going to be spelling detectives. You have a number of words which have got *ch* or *tch* in them, I want you to:
    (*a*) think of a number of other words which contain ch and tch,
    (*b*) divide the words into two lists, those with ch in and those with tch in,
    (*c*) try to work out if there is a rule which will help us to spell these words – to know when we should use ch and when tch.'

4. While the pupils are discussing, the teacher may wander round the groups listening and offering additional guidance where necessary. For instance, he may

    (*i*) suggest the pupils subdivide the words further according to whether ch occurs at the beginning, middle or end of words,
    (*ii*) prompt by suggesting they look at critical pairs – catch/coach, match/march – a powerful technique in inductive rule-finding,
    (*iii*) if they cannot find an all-embracing rule, suggest they look for a rule which covers *most* of the words and treat the others as exceptions. (It may be that one or more of the exceptions – such, rich, much, which – has

crept into their lists; indeed, with an able or older group the teacher might well slip one of these into the sample list.)

5. Each group appoints a spokesman to explain to the rest of the class what they have discovered, and after each group has reported, further class discussion ensues, or the teacher may draw together and summarize what they have found.

Wherever possible, then, children should be given the chance to at least investigate rules for themselves, not just because they will understand the particular rule better but also because they will acquire an insight into spelling as a rule-governed skill. Similarly, when devising practice exercises for the rule, the teacher should try to allow for some degree of initiative by the pupils. Rather than filling in gaps in sentences, or completing multiple choice exercises ('The candle was shinning/shining in the window'), the children might be asked to be more inventive:

Write a sentence using three of the following words: gnarled, gnash, gnat, gnaw, gnome.
Write a funny story about an elephant, using as many words containing ph as possible.
See how many words containing ie or ei you can get into a paragraph of five or six sentences.
Spot all the examples of 'magic e' in this passage.
Make up sentences where you get the particular rule wrong, e.g. The athlete was hopping for a fast time.

Teaching word-building

The English teacher may, occasionally, undertake vocabulary work on the meaning of prefixes and suffixes, and on the origins of words. This kind of word-analysis and word building has useful spin-offs for spelling. Looking at the way words are constructed out of their constituent parts can help a child to attack his own spelling demons. Some typical exercises might be:

(*a*) How many words can you make out of the following units? – re/dis/un arm/cover/order able/er/ing/ed. This selection presents no particular spelling problems, but units could be chosen to illustrate rules for the adding of suffixes, or changes in prefixes (incessant, impartial, illegal, irreversible).

(*b*) The 'random word-producer'. Pupils select prefixes, stems and suffixes to form their own new words – and then explain their meaning. This is the world where gruntled exearthlets discommunify round their retrovideotables.

Teaching homophones and similar pairs

A type of exercise which figures prominently in some English course-books is that which asks pupils to distinguish between homophones or other pairs of words which are often confused. Typical questions are:

Write two sentences to show the difference between 'affect' and 'effect'.

Choose the right word in the sentence: 'The boy shouted (allowed/aloud) in his nightmare.'

Pick out the errors in the sentence: 'The bells were wrung with a merry peel.'

The real purpose of these exercises is obscure, but one suspects they are usually aimed at vocabulary testing. That this is so is suggested by the inclusion of pairs where spelling is not an issue. (Write pairs of sentences to bring out two different meanings of 'refuse'; explain the difference between cónvict/convíct.) Whether or not they do fulfil any useful function in vocabulary work, these exercises should certainly be used very sparingly in connection with spelling. Generally, as we have seen, words likely to be confused should be treated separately, alongside other words spelt in the same way; treating them together can be very confusing for the pupil who is unsure of their spelling. Only if a pupil has thoroughly mastered the spelling of at least one of the pair should the exercise be attempted – and in that case there seems little point in doing it. An exception might be made for humorous errors, when the effect might be striking enough to 'fix' the spelling.

> He heard a horse whisper behind him.
> She pulled her male through the letter-box.
> The salmon went to the canary to be caned.

Teacher-initiated spellings

It was suggested earlier that, while marking pupils' work, the teacher keep some kind of record of their more important spelling errors. As he looks over this record, he may sometimes feel that he should take the initiative in suggesting words which the whole class should learn, even though there will always be some for whom this is unnecessary. Or important words may crop up during the course of other English work: judge, judicial, criminal, burglar, illegal, court – arising from a theme on law and order; armour, challenge, spear, warrior – from a novel being read; simile, metaphor, metaphorical, poetic – on the grounds that if we're going to talk about them we might as well be able to spell them, and a special bonus for anyone who manages 'onomatopoeia' next Friday.

There is no reason why subject teachers other than English should not make use of the pupils' spelling books, especially if the school has an 'across the curriculum' writing policy. One school which has such a policy, under the heading 'spelling' gives guidance to teachers on marking spelling errors in pupils' work, and concludes:

> Subject-specific words: subject teachers responsible for correct spelling of these. *Either* key words should be given to pupils in duplicated or dictated form to go onto a special

page before the unit of work in which they are likely to occur *or* they should be given to pupils when they crop up and written on a special page. Words subsequently spelt wrongly should be entered on a special page in the spelling book.

One teacher used 'spelling posters' with first- and second-year classes. She placed round the form room a number of posters illustrating common sources of spelling error (for example, doubled letters, vowel combinations). Each poster had an envelope underneath in which children could place their own examples of words which gave them trouble, and these were added to the poster by the teacher. Another method which can be used with the younger forms is to give the class two sentences to learn each week, each sentence being constructed so as to illustrate a particular spelling point:

The gnarled gnome gnashed his teeth as he gnawed the gnat.
The soldier seized the weird witch and threw her over the weir.

No matter the sense, if the picture be striking enough. A variant of this is for the teacher to designate a 'spellword' for the day or five 'magic words' for the week. When challenged by the teacher, a pupil must spell the word correctly or some horrible punishment ensues. Or the class could be challenged to use the words as often as possible in their own written work during the week, correctly spelt, of course. The teacher himself may tell children he is in the habit of making one deliberate spelling mistake each day, and they are to try to spot it.

Spelling games

It may be inferred from the above that spelling with the whole class should be a lively, even lighthearted affair. Indeed there are a variety of games, puzzles and similar activities which a teacher may draw upon if he wishes.

Spelling quizzes. The class is divided into teams and the teacher asks spelling questions of each child in turn, based on words he has given them to learn or words commonly misspelt. The team with the most points wins. As a scoring variation, 2 points may be given for a correct spelling and a word spelt incorrectly is passed over to the other teams (or the other members of his own team) for a bonus point.

Spelling bees. Here the children choose which words to ask – the person asking may or may not be challenged to spell the word himself. A particularly useful variant of this is for the teams to be 'paired off', each member of a pair having his partner's personal spelling book (and perhaps his personal dictionary) to select words from.

Spelling battles. A quiz or bee in which a player who spells a word wrongly is 'out' (or he could be given three chances – 'chipped, cracked and broken'). Alternatively he is 'captured' by the opposing team and continues to take part in the game.

Spelling rounders. Instead of 'pitching' a ball, one team 'pitches' words to be spelled by the other team. Members of the teams take it in turns to pitch and spell. If the word is correctly spelled the speller moves to first base, if his next team mate spells correctly the first man moves on to second base, and so on until a rounder is completed. The teacher may decide to allow one, two or three 'strikes' at a word before a player is adjudged to be out.

Call my bluff. Teams take it in turns to contribute letters to a word, but must avoid actually completing a word. For instance team A starts 'v', team B goes 've' (thinking of 'vegetable'), team C goes 'ive' (thinking of 'live') and team D goes 'rive' (thinking of 'river'). But they are challenged by team B, a dictionary is consulted, and they lose a point since 'rive' is a word. (Had it not been, team B would have lost a point.) Any team may 'call the bluff' of another team by challenging them to spell the word they are thinking of, a point being lost by whichever team loses the challenge. Incomplete words must be either the beginning or end of a word — 'ghou' can be justified by 'ghoul' but not by 'yoghourt'.

In all these games it is desirable for children to write the words, preferably on the blackboard, rather than spell them orally. In 'Call my bluff' the teacher can build up the words on the blackboard.

Word activities

Crosswords. These may be set by the teacher or devised by the children. Instead of complete crosswords, children can solve or invent crossword-type clues, e.g. anagrams or hidden words —

Divide up to see a part.	SEPARATE
The cab lacked colour.	BLACK

Fives. Clues are given to five words beginning or ending with the same letter or group of letters. The class may be told what the letters are or they may have to guess. Tricky spellings, difficult prefixes or suffixes, can be included.

a twin-hulled sailing-boat	CATAMARAN
an instrument of punishment in former times	CAT O' NINE TAILS
a special kind of church	CATHEDRAL
a tricky way of getting out	CATCH
a tool or dupe of someone	CATSPAW

Note that there should be some straightforward clues at the beginning if children are being asked to guess the key letters.

a bump in a car	DENT
the leader of the USA	PRESIDENT
to stop or hinder	PREVENT
standing on your own two feet	INDEPENDENT
a verbal dispute	ARGUMENT

No score for incorrect spelling!

Word squares. See worksheet exercise 4, p. 66.

Word targets. How many words can you make from the letters of TRAMPLE? (score points according to the number and length of words – so PART scores 5, 1 for the word and 4 for the letters.)

Word building. There are several varieties:

(a) I – in – sin – sing – string – staring – starling – startling.

(b) Get from BIRD to CAGE in 4 moves, changing one letter at a time, each change forming a word.

(c) Hangman. This can be played in pairs, or with the whole class, when the teacher can select words whose spelling presents difficulty.

(d) Shannon's game. Similar to hangman but children must guess the letters in order, i.e. having guessed the first letter, they must then guess the second, and so on.

Hunt the demon. Children work on passages in which one or more words are misspelt. The object is to spot the words and look up the correct spelling in a dictionary.

In addition to these suggestions there are many other games designed for or adaptable to spelling – scrabble, lexicon, spelling bingo – the teacher need never be at a loss for end of term activities!

Creative spelling

As suggested in an earlier section, there is ample opportunity for pupils to 'play' with spelling themselves, for instance by inventing sentences in which the use of the wrong word creates a humorous effect. Spoonerisms and puns provide a fruitful field for ingenuity and, indeed, underlie much schoolchild humour.

Another possibility is for the teacher to collect (anonymous) misspellings from pupils and get the class to invent meanings for them. 'Grimely' doesn't exist but perhaps it ought to (to describe the play of the local football team?), and 'coffing' sounds a thoroughly nefarious activity.

The use of nonsense words can help to emphasize the relationships between sound and symbol which underlie English spelling. For instance, the teacher says a nonsense word, and the pupils think of different ways to spell it. So, we might have: greable, greeble, grieble, greble (what spelling rule does this illustrate?), and also greabol and perhaps even greabal (by analogy with which words?), but what about greabul and ghreable? The children will see that, though there are usually different possibilities for spelling a word, the possibilities are not infinite, and some spellings are much more probable than others. One could go on from here to illustrate word building: if greable is a verb – 'Birds greable in the mating season' – how do we form the past tense and present participle: if greable is an adjective – 'A greable man is but a paltry thing' – how do we form the adverb, or the abstract noun ending in -ness, or the comparative and superlative?

One final area in which we can tap the creativity of pupils is to seek their help in suggesting mnemonics for remembering spelling. How, for instance, do they remember the stationery/ stationary distinction? The whole class may be involved in discussion of how to remember spelling rules – to the extent that one class were encouraged to declare in unison 'LICE!' whenever an 'ie' word appeared on the blackboard.

Spelling and language study

For the teacher who is interested in the history of languages, and the English language in particular, and who is curious about words, the study of spelling is a fascinating topic in itself. A number of themes can be explored with pupils, not as an attempt to improve pupils' spelling, but as part of that general awareness of and interest in language which many English teachers will wish to promote.

1. Alphabets, the history of written language, the origins

and development of our own alphabet, different methods of writing.

2.   Spelling and pronunciation, English spelling in earlier times (e.g. Chaucer, Shakespeare), leading to:

(*a*) phonetic notation, phonemic scripts (such as the initial teaching alphabet), spelling reform (this can spark off a lively discussion),

(*b*) sound changes in English and the development of 'unphonetic' spelling,

(*c*) dialects and the emergence of a 'standard' written English,

(*d*) the difficulty of English pronunciation and spelling for foreigners. (The verse 'Hints on pronunciation for foreigners' [see Appendix II, p. 182] might be used, and children invited to produce their own 'hints' for other spelling oddities.)

3.   The history of the English vocabulary, borrowings from other languages, the origins of words – some pupils may become fascinated by unusual spellings and their origins.

4.   English worldwide – differences between 'English' English and American, Scots and Australian English. Among other things this will help to put across the idea that English spelling is not something sacred and immutable.

5.   Alternative spellings – there are at least a hundred fairly common words for which alternative spellings are perfectly permissible. This might also include a discussion of the spelling of advertising slogans: Drinka Pinta Milka Day, Beanz Meanz Heinz. Is *this* permissible?

6.   Does spelling matter? This is a topic well worth raising with older pupils. What do they think? Why does it matter? Whereabouts in a hierarchy of language priorities would they place good spelling? A unit on spelling might form part of a wider theme on language varieties and what constitutes 'good' English.

6

TEACHING PUNCTUATION*

Teaching punctuation to individuals

There are two reasons why helping pupils individually to improve their punctuation is likely to prove the most effective long-term strategy. In any class, especially a mixed-ability class, pupils' needs are likely to be very different. Attempting to teach the 'use of the apostrophe' to a typical second-year class, for instance, one may expect that a number of children will already be using the apostrophe accurately, some children may have such major problems with their writing that any attempt to 'improve' their use of the apostrophe is entirely misplaced, and the remainder may be making many different kinds of error: invariably using 's even when the word is plural (boy's school); using s' in words like mens', childrens'; sometimes using 's and sometimes not; using 's for ordinary plurals (boy's and girl's come out to play); putting ' in the

* Single inverted commas for direct speech and double inverted commas for quotations within direct speech have been used throughout, in accordance with the publisher's house style. The author recognizes that teachers will almost certainly advise children to use double inverted commas for speech.

wrong place (would'nt, shel'l); using ' in possessive pronouns (it's, their's, her's). These errors have different causes and need different remedies; any class instruction is likely to miss the mark for all but a few children.

A second and more important reason for advocating individual help is that pupils learn best when the teaching is addressed to their own individual problems, when it meets a need which they can see relates to their own written work. Perhaps the chief reason why punctuation exercises have so little effect in improving pupils' written work is that they are seen as artificial and isolated – they don't give concentrated practice where the pupil needs it most. A second drawback is that such exercises tend to stress 'correct' punctuation, whereas in commenting on the work of an individual pupil a teacher is able to emphasize the *positive* contribution of punctuation, by pointing out ways in which punctuation can help to make the writing more effective.

The first stage in improving punctuation is to note where a pupil needs help and to discuss briefly with him what he needs to do. This may happen as a result of a piece of work the teacher has marked, or as a part of the 'writing workshops' when children are working on their rough drafts in class. The following essay, by a first year pupil, illustrates a fairly typical punctuation error at that age.

The Day the Monkey Escaped

On Friday Mr Greaves bought his pet monkey to school. It escaped during assembley and ran into the hall, it was packet with children, the headmaster was making his speach. The monkey jumped up, it swung on the lights, every body watched in surprise....

People tried to catch the monkey, it got noisier and noisier. It jumped on to the piano making a loud crashing noise, every body laughed....

(Hector, age 12)

Although this particular error of 'run-on' sentences tends to clear itself up in time, the teacher may judge it helpful to talk to Hector about his work. He could for instance, ask Hector to read the essay aloud, slowly and carefully — a very useful technique which often has the effect of making children realize for themselves that their punctuation impedes communication. The teacher could help Hector to listen to the pauses and intonation, and to decide where the full-stops ought to be placed. Or he might offer an explanation in terms of each sentence expressing one main idea, unless it is joined to another sentence in some way. This suggests an alternative approach, of restructuring the sentence rather than tampering with the punctuation, so preserving the intentions of the writer, who evidently often uses a comma to indicate a connection which is not explicitly expressed, e.g.:

> It escaped during assembly and ran into the hall, which was packed with children listening to the headmaster's speech. Everybody watched in surprise as/when the monkey jumped up and swung on the lights.
> It got noisier and noisier as people tried to catch the monkey.
> Everybody laughed as it jumped onto the piano making a loud crashing noise.

Whatever line the teacher takes, the important thing is that some explanation is offered to Hector and he is given some help in getting it right next time.

The second stage in helping individual pupils is to provide immediate practice to reinforce the particular point of punctuation. As with spelling, such practice may be undertaken in odd moments or at home so as not to occupy a disproportionate amount of class time. In Hector's case, he might get together with another child needing similar help. Working with a tape recorder, they read extracts from their essays, listen carefully to the pauses and intonation, and decide where the full stops should be placed. Again as with spelling, the teacher may find it useful to have a workcard system, whereby common errors can be coded and the child referred to a particular workcard for practice. For instance, referring to Andrew's essay (Chapter 5, p. 56) the teacher might wish to direct Andrew's attention to the proper setting-out of direct speech. Using the appropriate code, Andrew is sent to a workcard and accompanying worksheet.

SPEECH 2

'I know what it is,' said Peter; 'it's a beaver. I saw the tail.' 'It wants us to go to it,' said Susan, 'and it is warning us not to make a noise.' 'I know,' said Peter. 'The question is, are we to go to it or not? What do you think, Lu?' 'I think it's a nice beaver,' said Lucy. 'Yes, but how do we *know*?' said Edmund. 'Shan't we have to risk it?' said Susan. (C. S. Lewis, *The Lion, the Witch and the Wardrobe*.)

.This conversation is difficult to read. It ought to be set out:

'I know what it is,' said Peter; 'it's a beaver. I saw the tail.'

'It wants us to go to it,' said Susan, 'and it is warning us not to make a noise.'

'I know,' said Peter. 'The question is, are we to go to it or not? What do you think, Lu?'

'I think it's a nice beaver,' said Lucy.

'Yes, but how do we *know*?' said Edmund.

'Shan't we have to risk it?' said Susan.

Rule A new speaker needs a new paragraph.

Andrew is asked to read the workcard and copy the rule and the correctly punctuated passage into his punctuation note-book. Note that the workcard deals with only one point of punctuation – punctuation conventions should be broken down into small steps, each card dealing with one step only. The worksheets give cumulative practice in the new point and all those which have gone before. For instance, a full range of speech workcards might read:

SPEECH 1 Use of inverted commas round words actually spoken.

SPEECH 2 Paragraphing of direct speech.

SPEECH 3 Other punctuation marks (full-stop, question mark, exclamation mark) in speech.

SPEECH 4 A new sentence in speech needs a capital letter.

SPEECH 5 Comma before direct speech – verb of saying at beginning.

SPEECH 6 Comma after direct speech – verb of saying at end.

SPEECH 7 Broken sentences in direct speech – verb of saying in middle.

SPEECH 8 When the speech is more than one sentence – verb of saying in middle as a special case.

SPEECH 9 When the whole sentence is a question or exclamation – punctuation marks outside inverted commas.

SPEECH 10 Using two sets of inverted commas – quotations, titles, etc. in direct speech.

SPEECH 11 Placing of other punctuation marks when two sets of inverted commas are used.

SPEECH 12 Turning reported speech into direct speech.

SPEECH 13 Turning direct speech into reported speech.

It will be observed that these speech workcards span the whole of the secondary school age-range and would be referred to at different times: 1 to 4 are fairly basic and should be mastered by most first- and second-year pupils, 5 to 8 are more technical and might be taken up by second- and third-year pupils as the need arises, 9 to 11 would be more appropriate for fourth- and fifth-year pupils, while 12 and 13 might only be used if an external examination asked for these particular skills.

Having looked at the workcard, Andrew turns to the worksheet for practice.

SPEECH 2   WORKSHEET

1 Look at the cartoon below, then write out the conversation, beginning

   Albert greeted his friend, Peter. 'Hello, four eyes, hello ...'

   Make sure (*i*) You put any words spoken between inverted commas,

   (*ii*) each new speaker begins a new paragraph.

2 Below is a short extract from a play. Write it out as a conversation, using inverted commas and putting in suitable 'saying' words. Include stage directions as part of the story.

MEGAERA: (*suddenly throwing down her stick*) I won't go another step.

ANDROCLES: (*pleading wearily*) Oh, not again, dear. We must get on to the next village before night. There are wild beasts in this wood: lions, they say.

M: I don't believe a word of it. We haven't seen a single lion yet.

A: Well, dear, do you want to see one?

M: (*tearing the bundle from his back and throwing it on the ground*) You don't care what becomes of me: always thinking of yourself. Self! Self! always yourself! (*She sits down on the bundle.*)

A: (*sitting down sadly on the ground*) We all have to think of ourselves occasionally, dear.

M: A man ought to think of his wife sometimes.

A: He can't always help it, dear. You make me think of you a good deal. Not that I blame you.

M: Blame me! I should think not indeed. Is it my fault that I am married to you?

A: No, dear: that is my fault.

(Adapted from G. B. Shaw, *Androcles and the Lion*)

3 Below is a muddled conversation between a store detective and a shoplifter. Write it out in the proper order, paragraphing correctly.

'What is this camera doing here, madam?' 'Why, what do you want to look for?' 'What nonsense! Of course you can look.' 'Excuse me, madam, may I look in your bag?' 'I'm afraid I must ask you to accompany me to the manager's office.' 'I don't know. It must have fallen off the shelf into my bag.' 'I believe you have goods which you haven't paid for.'

4 There are three mistakes in the following passage. Write it out correctly.

'Have you done your homework?' asked the English teacher.
'No, said John, I had to go out last night.'
'Where to?' 'I went to the theatre with my parents.'
'Don't believe him, sir,' interrupted Algy.
'He was watching football on television.'

5 Choose one of the following situations:

   (*a*) A policeman stopping a man carrying a suspicious-looking bag.

   (*b*) Two friends discussing what they will do on a day's holiday from school.

   (*c*) You trying to convince your parents you should have more pocket-money.

Write out the conversation which takes place, using direct speech.

When constructing workcards and worksheets, the teacher may find it useful to consult a sound manual on punctuation (see the Appendix for some suggestions) and also coursebooks containing punctuation exercises.

The third stage in helping individual pupils is to monitor the improvement in punctuation in their own writing, by continuing to remind pupils of the need to check punctuation in final drafts, and by commenting favourably on the effective use of punctuation. The reward for both teacher and pupil is to see a gradual development in the accurate and flexible deployment of punctuation.

Teaching punctuation to the class

Although the main thrust of punctuation teaching will be directed to improving the work of individual pupils, some class teaching of punctuation will be necessary. Occasionally an error will be common enough in pupils' work to warrant attention with the whole class. Additionally, a teacher may decide to raise with a class a use of punctuation which is new or unfamiliar to them. This is especially the case with the more esoteric punctuation marks, such as colon or semi-colon, or the rarer uses such as the apostrophe to indicate abbreviated plurals – 'mind your P's and Q's', 'in the 1870's'. Unless such conventions are brought directly to the pupils' notice it is difficult to see how they could ever become adept in their use. Most often of all, a teacher may decide to summarize for the class a good deal of incidental, individual teaching which they may have experienced previously. For instance, during the third year a teacher may wish to summarize and make explicit the conventions governing the use of other punctuation marks in direct speech (covered by the speech workcards 3–8).

Generally a teacher will not want to spend more than about ten to fifteen minutes in any one lesson on punctuation activities. A useful technique is to enlist the co-operation of the class in short sessions of blackboard work.

SECOND YEAR

The teacher writes on the board short phrases which pupils volunteer (or are volunteered!) to turn into the possessive, placing the apostrophe where they think it should go.

the book belonging to the boy	the boy's book
the school for boys	the boys' school
a story for children	a children's story

After each one, the class are invited to spot any errors and the teacher stresses the technique of looking back at the original phrase to see whether the apostrophe is correctly placed. Now some possessives are written up, and children come out to put in the apostrophe – the princess dress; the princesses dresses; the mens hats – and the class encouraged to check by expanding the phrase ('the hats of the mens'?).

FOURTH YEAR

The teacher writes on the board:

John said, 'He sang "Where did the Snowman Go"'
John asked, 'Did he sing "Happy Birthday"'
Did John say, 'He sang "Happy Birthday"'

and the pupils are invited to insert question marks in the appropriate place.

The teacher now poses: Did John ask, 'Did he sing "Where did the Snowman Go"' This always produces a lively discussion, not to mention incredulity at the final result.

A number of similar short exercises can be undertaken with the whole class to reinforce or emphasize particular punctuation points:

(*i*) inserting punctuation marks which have been omitted (the omissions may or may not be indicated in some way);

(*ii*) correcting punctuation errors – as a variant of this the teacher may be in the habit of making the occasional deliberate error for the pupils to spot;

(*iii*) explaining (or justifying, or criticizing) the use of particular punctuation marks;

(*iv*) resolving ambiguity by the use of punctuation marks, or discussing instances where a change in punctuation alters the meaning. For instance, what are the two possible meanings of

> That boy said Mr Smedley is a fool.
> At the disco I met Jane and her brother Mark came later.

and how should they be punctuated in each case? How can we punctuate to clarify the meaning of 'Charles where James had had had had had had had had had had pleased the examiner better'? Pupils might be encouraged to bring into the classroom newspaper or magazine clippings in which there is faulty or ambiguous punctuation.

All I am suggesting here is that teachers spend short periods in lessons to reinforce points of punctuation in a lively and interesting way, involving the whole class. Occasionally a longer exercise in altering punctuation may be set, perhaps as part of a wider proof-reading or 'improving' exercise, working, say, on an imaginary children's letter or an (anonymous) piece of work written by a pupil. Again, as part of their own proof-reading children can be encouraged to exchange work in pairs and pay special attention to the use of (particular marks of) punctuation, so that one child might have to justify his use of, say, commas to his partner.

Strange Tappings in the Early Hours

It was early in the morning when John woke up. He looked at the time wondering whether to get up and then, realising it was about 5.30. he started to doze off. Then the tapping started. It went on and off sometimes quiet sometimes loud until John got out of bed and the tapping stopped.... During the day John did various jobs around the house and, when cleaning the car his dad told him that "some daft bird" had been attacking its reflection in the car mirror.

(Jackie, age 13)

This story is used by the teacher with a third-year class for a discussion of commas. First he asks them all to write it out themselves, inserting commas, then, in pairs, to check each other's versions and agree, if they can, on a correct version. Finally, they contribute their ideas to a class discussion. The following points emerge during the discussion:

(*i*) sometimes, commas are needed in pairs to separate off phrases from the main sentence: wondering whether to get up, realizing it was about 5.30, when cleaning the car,

(*ii*) sometimes commas are needed to indicate a pause in reading a sentence: on and off, sometimes quiet, sometimes loud,

(*iii*) sometimes the use of a comma is optional: during the day, John...

Punctuation and speech

Since many punctuation conventions represent in writing features of the spoken language, one valuable task a teacher can perform is to help pupils understand the relationship between punctuation and the spoken language. They can investigate the importance of punctuation by trying to read aloud passages with no punctuation, or with particular punctuation marks (perhaps full-stops and commas) omitted, or with a full-stop inserted arbitrarily after, say, every seven words. They can tape-record and listen to their efforts. What problems do we have interpreting a passage with no punctuation marks? Why does a news-reader need to practise his reading beforehand? Pupils can listen to tape-recordings, attempt to transcribe them, and discuss what resources we can use in speech which we do not have available in writing. They will notice features of intonation, stress, pitch and loudness; the way the dialogue is paced, including pauses and silences; voice quality like warmth, laughter, sarcasm, harshness. They can begin to realize that punctuation, along with word-order and typographical features, is a major way of capturing the nuances of spoken language. Intonation is especially significant. (Listening to a reading of the football results provides a good introduction to intonation. Arsenal 1 Chelsea? – we already know whether Chelsea scored 0, 1 or more than 1 goal. How?) It may be helpful to develop with pupils a very simple notation for the contours of intonation, describing the 'shape' of the basic sentence patterns. These can then be related to the 'sentence' punctuation marks: full-stop, comma, question mark and exclamation mark – so that children can describe the intonation patterns of the following sentences:

You haven't forgotten your homework. (I'm glad to see.)
You haven't forgotten your homework? (Have you?)
You haven't forgotten your homework! (I don't believe it.)

Or pupils can listen for the characteristic intonation patterns, combined with the length of pause, which distinguish the following sentences and indicate whether comma, full-stop or no punctuation mark is needed.

The girl passed by her teacher. //
The girl passed by her teacher // without noticing him.
The girl passed by her teacher // and ran to her friends.
The girl passed by her teacher // failed the examination.

In each of these sentences, if we stop at //, we are caught in a different intonation pattern.

Punctuation and reading

Opportunities to discuss punctuation with the whole class may occur incidentally during English lessons. Reading dialogue in a class novel affords a good opportunity for reinforcing the conventions of direct speech, especially if children are chosen to read the different characters.

A second-year class are reading *The Hobbit* when this dialogue occurs in Chapter 5.

'Where is it? Where iss it?' Bilbo heard him crying. 'Losst it is, my precious, lost, lost! Curse us and crush us, my precious is lost!'

'What's the matter?' Bilbo called. 'What have you lost?'

'It mustn't ask us,' shrieked Gollum. 'Not its business, no, gollum! It's lost, gollum, gollum, gollum.'

'Well, so am I,' cried Bilbo, 'and I want to get unlost. And I won the game, and you promised. So come along! Come and let me out, and then go on with your looking!' Utterly miserable as Gollum sounded, Bilbo could not find much pity in his heart, and he had a feeling that anything Gollum wanted so much could hardly be something good. 'Come along!' he shouted.

'No, not yet, precious!' Gollum answered. 'We must search for it, it's lost, gollum.'

'But you never guessed my last question, and you promised,' said Bilbo.

'Never guessed!' said Gollum. Then suddenly out of the gloom came a sharp hiss. 'What has it got in its pocketses? Tell us that. It must tell first.'

(J. R. R. Tolkien, *The Hobbit*, Chapter 5)

The teacher allocates the parts of Gollum and Bilbo to two children, with the instruction (which they are used to) that they read only the words actually spoken. This reinforces the use of inverted commas to separate direct speech from the main narrative and the use of paragraphs to indicate different speakers. Additionally the class discuss briefly how the dialogue should be spoken, paying attention to words like 'crying', 'shrieked', 'miserable', 'sharp hiss'. This leads on to the more important question of what kind of a creature Gollum is, and what our feelings towards him are. The teacher does not interrupt the flow of the lesson to discuss punctuation specifically, but ten minutes from the end of the lesson she returns to this passage and selects two sentences from it. ('Well so am I', cried Bilbo, 'and I want to get unlost.' 'What's the matter?' Bilbo called. 'What have you lost?') She writes the sentences on the board, and uses them to discuss the punctuation of broken sentences in direct speech.

The teacher may also draw attention to the creative use of punctuation by writers – how punctuation can be used to contribute to the effectiveness of a piece of writing. Dickens especially often used punctuation in an idiosyncratic manner to achieve particular effects:

'Davy, dear. If I ain't been azackly as intimate with you. Lately, as I used to be. It ain't because I don't love you. Just as well and more, my pretty poppet. It's because I thought it better for you. And for someone else besides.'

(*David Copperfield*, Chapter 4)

'Take the book in your right hand this is your name and
handwriting you swear that the contents of this your
affidavit are true so help you God a shilling you must get
change I haven't got it.'

(*Pickwick Papers*, Chapter 40)

If a teacher has recently dealt with the semi-colon, and the
class are reading *David Copperfield*, what better than to
consider how Dickens uses the semi-colon:

Undulating hills were changed to valleys, undulating valleys
(within a solitary storm-bird sometimes skimming through
them) were lifted up as hills; masses of water shivered and
shook the beach with a booming sound; every shape
tumultuously rolled on, as soon as made, to change its
shape and place, and beat another shape and place away;
the ideal shore on the horizon, with its towers and
buildings, rose and fell; the clouds flew fast and thick; I
seemed to see a rending and upheaving of all nature.

(*David Copperfield*, Chapter 55)

I suppose the question to ask is what difference it would make
if Dickens had used full-stops instead of semi-colons. Pupils
can see how the punctuation, working together with the
syntax, achieves a 'piling-up' of clauses suggesting the relent-
lessness and overwhelming force of the storm.

Teaching specific punctuation marks

SENTENCE PUNCTUATION

I don't suppose any pupil, by the time he reaches secondary
school, needs to be told that sentences begin with a capital
letter and end with a full stop. Very likely he has been told this
many times at primary school, has been warned to 'watch
your full-stops', and may even have suffered interminable

exercises of the 'add full-stops and capital letters' or 'turn the following into complete sentences' variety. The problem is to know when a sentence begins and ends. This depends on a fairly sophisticated sentence awareness which even adults might find difficult to make explicit. Definitions such as 'a sentence makes complete sense' tend to be circular (how do we know what makes complete sense?) and in any case miss the point – we don't want children to stop every few seconds to puzzle about whether a group of words 'makes complete sense'. We must help children develop an intuitive 'feel' for sentences. Some techniques for doing this were suggested earlier in connection with Hector's essay (p. 84). It is best done on an individual basis, getting the child to listen to the pauses and intonation patterns in his writing, or developing sentence awareness through his restructuring the sentences in his own work.

A class activity which works well with younger pupils is 'scrambled sentences'. The teacher writes sentences on a card, cutting up each sentence into three chunks. Each child is given an envelope containing three such sentences which they have to unscramble and write out in their books. The teacher first works one or two examples on the board and reminds them that every sentence must begin with a capital letter, end with a full stop, and make complete sense. A typical envelope might contain the cards for these sentences:

The convict/climbed over the prison wall/and escaped.
The children/went to the zoo/with their mother.
The birds/started to sing/early in the morning.

Children soon enter into the spirit of the exercise with sentences like 'The children climbed over the prison wall with their mother' or 'The convict started to sing and escaped'. The task can be varied for the abler pupils by cutting up longer sentences into four or five chunks, by missing off capital letters and full-stops, or by including one random chunk in each envelope and asking children to discover the intruder (for instance, 'if it rains' in the envelope described above).

The punctuation of sentences tends to improve as children gain more experience through reading and writing, and as their own written syntax develops. However, even older pupils may need individual help from time to time. Below is a paragraph written by Carol, a fourth-year pupil in a CSE set, from an essay on 'How I would improve the quality of life at my school'.

> The fourth point would be a sterner discipline, what is the use of putting people on report, that isn't really going to strike much terror into the person involved. Take for example a person who plays truant and he wants to scive a lesson all he needs do is get some tracing paper trace the last signature given to him by the teacher who's lesson he will be missing and fill in the blank spaces. I think more harsh punishment should be given eg, the cane.

The essay has been written in a lively, colloquial style, and has been punctuated accordingly. The teacher thought it appropriate to spend a few minutes with Carol getting her to read the passage slowly, listening to the pauses and intonation patterns to determine where full stops and commas should be placed. Another approach would be to ask the class to redraft their essays as formal letters of 'suggestions' to the headmaster. Carol could then be helped to restructure her sentences in a less colloquial manner:

4. Discipline should be sterner. Putting people on report is not a very effective punishment. If a person who plays truant wants to miss a lesson, all he needs to do is ...

The use of capital letters for 'proper nouns', titles, etc. is purely conventional and not entirely consistent (why do days of the week have capitals but not names of seasons?), and can be dealt with on an individual basis if necessary. The conventions for use of the full-stop for abbreviations are worth pointing out, and questions on abbreviations might be included in language games or general knowledge quizzes, but are not otherwise worth spending much time on.

COMMAS

With commas we enter the realm of stylistic choice, since often the decision whether to use a comma or not is a matter of judgement and personal preference rather than hard-and-fast rules. Although some textbooks describe over twenty uses of the comma, two broad principles should suffice to guide children in their use of this flexible mark.

(*i*) Commas are used to make things easier to read. They signal short pauses, separate long stretches of writing which would otherwise be confusing – in general, help to clarify the meaning. As with full-stops, the best approach is to encourage children to read their work carefully, thinking where commas are needed and would be helpful to the reader. This principle encompasses the use of commas to separate items in a list (of words, phrases, or clauses):

Second-year, mixed ability
The teacher writes on the board the sentence: 'She shopped at Tesco Marks and Spencer and Sainsbury and bought bread rolls eggs butter mustard and cress', and asks the class where commas ought to be placed so as to make it easier to read. The discussion highlights the potential ambiguity, if commas are omitted, of 'bread rolls' and 'Marks and Spencer' v. 'Spencer and Sainsbury'. The teacher asks how we know it is 'mustard/cress' rather than 'mustard and cress'. The children are then given three similar lists to punctuate themselves.

Children can be encouraged to discuss and justify the use of commas in their own and other people's writing, since it *is* so often a matter of style.

(*ii*) Commas are used to indicate sentence structure by separating off words, phrases or clauses which are incidental to the main sentence. A very common mistake is to use only one comma when a pair is needed, and pupils should be introduced, certainly by the third year, to this useful concept of 'bracketing off' by the use of commas. There are various ways of emphasizing this, for instance actually using brackets, while some writers talk of a main track (the main sentence) and branch lines, or a main road and side roads. The bracketed word(s) can be moved around the sentence to show how sometimes one and sometimes a pair of commas is needed.

Third-year, mixed ability
The teacher writes three sentences on the board:

> (However) the train was late.
> The train (however) was late.
> The train was late (however).

He asks how these sentences should be punctuated, pointing out that the main sentence 'the train was late' can have 'however' added to it in different positions. He asks individual children to come out to the board and put brackets round the words added to the main sentence in further examples:

> Meanwhile the police unknown to the criminals had set an ambush.
> England lost the match because their key players both in midfield and in defence were out of form unfortunately.

Each bracket is then changed to a comma, except where the beginning or end of a sentence supervenes. The children spend ten minutes punctuating similar examples in rough, first using brackets then converting to commas. Finally the teacher uses the sentence 'However did you do it' to demonstrate that a bracketing comma can change the meaning:

> However did you do it!   However, did you do it?

More generally, pupils can be encouraged to use colour, underlining, and other graphical devices to indicate the structure of sentences. For instance, they could write out the following sentence in its two possible meanings, showing which is the 'main line' and which the 'branch line' in each case, and then insert the commas.

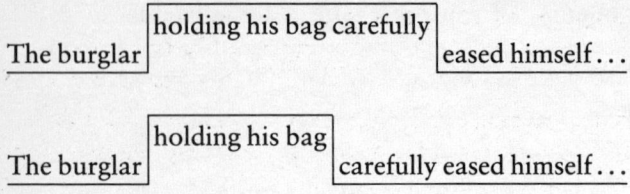

The burglar, holding his bag carefully, eased himself
through the open window.
The burglar, holding his bag, carefully eased himself
through the open window.

Often the decision whether to use no commas at all or a pair of bracketing commas is a matter of style – what is *not* permissible, however, is to use just one comma when a pair is needed. This is a point worth discussing with pupils, as are the cases where the use or omission of commas changes the meaning. A tricky point to grasp but one which should be raised with older pupils is the use of commas with defining and non-defining adjective clauses (without, of course, necessarily using the nomenclature). So, a fourth-year class might be invited to discuss the difference in meaning between pairs like:

The boys who had forgotten their homework were
   punished.
The boys, who had forgotten their homework, were
   punished.

Commas are a fruitful source of mispunctuation or ambiguous punctuation in newspapers, and both teachers and pupils might bring in examples for discussion.

'All members of the crew, normally about 270 strong, who abandoned ship, were picked up.' Were all members of the crew rescued or not? (In fact, as the article goes on to make plain, several were lost.) Why, then, has the comma been placed after 'ship'?

'The judge ruled that the will was contrary to marriage law and reduced the bequest

− to the wife.
− to the mistress.'

What is the likely meaning of each of these two sentences? Would a comma after 'law' help to clarify the meaning?

In general, it is probably best not to fuss too much about misuse of commas in pupils' written work, but to stress that this is a punctuation mark which can be used with discretion to improve the effectiveness of communication.

PUNCTUATING SPEECH

The punctuation of direct speech was discussed earlier (pp. 86–90), and appropriate exercises suggested. It is worth repeating that punctuating speech is quite a complex task which should be broken down, dealt with a point at a time, and returned to at intervals throughout the secondary curriculum. The essential features, which should be stressed from the beginning, are the use of inverted commas for words actually spoken, and the separation of speakers into separate paragraphs − since these conventions make for greater ease of reading. Other, more technical features, such as the use of other punctuation marks in direct speech, can be delayed until later, at least as far as class instruction is concerned. Punctuation of direct speech can be incorporated into the general writing activities of the English programme:

First-year, mixed ability

The teacher introduces the class to the topic of unlikely excuses. She describes how she once had to miss an examination because a jar of pickled onions fell on her head in the middle of the night − and the general scepticism with which her excuse was greeted. (She explains that she awoke feeling hungry and went downstairs to raid the pantry.) She invites the class to contribute other instances when they, or someone they know, had to offer or invent an unlikely excuse. She then writes on the board:

'Come here, boy!' roared the headmaster. 'Just why are you climbing through that window?'

She asks the class to continue the dialogue for another three or four exchanges on each side, and she reminds them of the following points: each new speaker gets a new paragraph; words actually spoken must be placed in inverted commas; other punctuation marks, such as the exclamation mark and question mark, should be placed inside the inverted commas. She explains that, when marking the work, she will pay special attention to the ingenuity of the excuse *and* the way in which the conversation is set out.

Fourth-year, CSE set

The pupils are carrying out a project for an imaginary Radio X, 'An in-depth profile of ... School'. Working in pairs they prepare interviews with a pupil, teacher, headmaster, parent or local resident. Each pair, when ready, tapes its interview, and a compilation is recorded to play to other classes in the school.

As part of the project, the class write a report on the programme for a local newspaper, each pair concentrating on a report of its own interview. After each pair has written a rough draft, the teacher asks them to list some of the differences between the direct speech of their interview and the reported speech of their newspaper account, and discusses with the class the main 'rules' for turning direct into reported speech. The class then produce a final draft of the article.

Third-year, second band

The class are reading *Elidor*, and the teacher directs their attention to the following passage.

> 'Have you messed up my transistor?' said Nicholas from the doorway. He was looking at David, and his face was hot.
>
> 'Why should I want to touch your puny transistor when I've built a real wireless of my own?' said David.
>
> 'Someone has,' said Nicholas. 'Is it either of you two?'
>
> 'Not me,' said Roland. 'What's wrong with it?'
>
> 'You listen,' said Nicholas. . . .
>
> (A. Garner, Elidor, Chapter 10)

The teacher asks the class for other words which might be used instead of the ubiquitous 'said', and the children look for examples in their library books (asked, inquired, demanded, answered, replied, insisted, etc.). For homework they are asked to write a story 'A strange meeting' or 'The quarrel', using direct speech and trying to vary as effectively as they can the 'saying' words.

APOSTROPHES

The apostrophe is probably a much over-taught punctuation mark. In modern English it is often an unnecessary convention. It is true that ambiguity can arise ('shell' or 'she'll', 'well' or 'we'll'; 'the boys school' – is it the school to which *that* boy goes [the boy's school], or the school for boys [the boys' school]?), but usually the context makes clear which is intended. It is better, in the early stages, to keep separate the two distinct uses of the apostrophe, for omission and to indicate possession. This kind of exercise, which one sometimes sees, is calculated to cause confusion:

> Insert apostrophes in the following sentences:
> 1. Its true that its lost its cover.
> 2. Ones aware that one can only do ones best.
> 3. Hes going to the library to change his book and hers.

The apostrophe for omission requires simply that children think where letters have been missed out. If a child writes 'shel'l' or 'ca'nt' he can be asked to work it out from the full version:

She will   She*ll   She'll
Cannot   Can*t   Can't

This is the time to deal with 'it's':

it is   it*s   it's

There are one or two irregularities such as won't or shan't, but these do not usually cause problems since the habit soon develops of inserting an apostrophe between 'n' and 't'. Older pupils can be introduced to more sophisticated examples such as will o' the wisp, nine o'clock, 'aint, 'phone, and can invent their own usages along the lines of 'fish 'n' chips', ' 'ave a cup o' (cuppa?) tea'.

It is the apostrophe for possession which causes most difficulty. Although the conventions are, in principle, clear-cut, they are often taught before children can really understand them and certainly before they can see the need to apply them. The main problem is that the -s ending is used for both plurals and possession; the combination of the two causes chronic confusion. The best method is for the teacher to provide carefully selected examples to help the children induce the rules for themselves, and to get children to check their possessives by looking back at the expanded form. We would suggest the following stages:

(*i*) singular possessives not ending in s and plural possess-ives ending in s

the books belonging to the *boy* = the ⎢boy⎢'s books

the books belonging to the *boys* = the ⎢boys⎢' books

the ⌐hen⌐'s eggs = the eggs laid by the *hen*

the ⌐hens⌐' eggs = the eggs laid by the *hens*

(*ii*) plural possessives not ending in s

a ⌐children⌐'s story = a story for *children*

The sheeps' tails – why is this wrong? – the tails of the *sheeps*

(*iii*) singular possessives ending in s . Here there is a genuine alternative, though 's is usually preferred when it is sounded

the bus's window was broken   St James's Church
(cf. the buses' windows were broken)

This technique helps to get right possessive pronouns such as 'ours', 'theirs' and 'yours' (we cannot say 'of our', 'of their', 'of your') but it does not help with 'hers' and 'its' which have to be learned separately. The best approach to apostrophes is to help individuals who need it, using a workcard and worksheet system, reinforced occasionally by brief class revision sessions (see p. 91). Personally, I would advocate a low-key approach to correcting apostrophe errors in the pupils' own written work; the most important thing is to stop pupils using an intrusive apostrophe is straightforward plurals (as is sometimes seen in shop windows: 'best quality apple's and orange's', 'two egg's and chip's'), and this is best done by not nagging them about omitted apostrophes.

With older pupils it is interesting to bring the two uses of the apostrophe together and show how the possessive use originated in the omission of 'e' from the genitive -es ending. This could be done as part of a wider study of change in the English language, perhaps by looking at extracts from Chaucer where the -es ending survives. Indeed, the origin of punctuation marks is an interesting topic in itself; pupils might like to find out about their origin, about the punctuation conventions used in other orthographies, and might even invent their own – punctuation marks which we *ought* to have.

The four features of punctuation so far discussed might be called 'basic' features – they are certainly the punctuation marks which will have received some attention in primary school. The remaining features are for the most part 'optional extras' – useful resources for a writer to have at his command, but not absolutely necessary. They can, therefore, safely be left to the older forms, and then introduced as additional aids to the effectiveness of communication, to be used at the writer's discretion.

COLONS AND SEMI-COLONS

These two marks are often taught together but, in fact, they are very different in meaning and utility. The colon is purely a convention, to be used when introducing a list of some kind, or a quotation – it is really equivalent to 'as follows', or 'namely' – and its use can be easily taught: preparing a list of instructions (for example, a recipe); writing notes in which items are summarized; making a statement and then adding illustrations or examples, as in this present sentence.

The semi-colon is a much more flexible punctuation mark, whose use is not easy to pin down since it depends so much on style. One can never point to an example where a semi-colon ought definitely to have been used; as in this sentence, it is always possible to punctuate in a different way. The two most common uses have already occurred in this section: to suggest a connection between what are syntactically two separate sentences, and to mark off the more important syntactic units in a complicated sentence which already uses a number of commas for less important breaks.

A brief explanation of the uses of the semi-colon might be given to third- or fourth-year pupils; thereafter opportunities may be taken to comment on the use of the semi-colon in books being read (see p. 97), or to suggest where individual pupils might have used it in their own writing (and to praise them when they use the semi-colon effectively). A fourth-year pupil, Simon, writes:

> The cane should be brought back and that would stop people being or behaving bad in lessons, it ought to be ruler for miner offences slipper for the next and the cane for the really bad offences.

The teacher discusses with Simon ways in which the sentence might be reconstructed or repunctuated and they agree that a semi-colon after 'lessons' would be the best solution.

DASHES AND BRACKETS

These can be dealt with at the same time as the 'bracketing' use of commas, since they are stylistic alternatives. The subtle differences in meaning can be discussed by examining a series like:

> The boy who had never sat an examination before was nervous.
> The boy, who had never sat an examination before, was nervous.
> The boy – who had never sat an examination before – was nervous.
> The boy (who had never sat an examination before) was nervous.

The single dash, used to make a sharp break in a sentence, or to tack on an afterthought, is another useful stylistic device. As with the semi-colon, the best procedure is to introduce these marks to the pupils and then keep an eye open for their use, or opportunities to use them, in the pupils' own writing. Occasionally, one could set an exercise asking pupils to concoct a short passage using as many different punctuation marks as possible, or to compose sentences using specified punctuation marks, provided this is done in a spirit of adventure!

HYPHENS

Sometimes the use of the hyphen *is* compulsory, especially to indicate compound words ('I saw a man-eating tiger'/'I saw a man eating pheasant'), but one has really to scrape the barrel to find genuine ambiguity – as so often, the context usually makes all clear.

> He hit one head high over the slips.
> She is a hard working woman.

Another use of the hyphen worth pointing out to pupils is to indicate word structure: re-form, co-operate, un-British, lamp-post; and perhaps pupils could have fun inventing their own compound words:

> He is a died-in-the-wool, hunting-and-shooting-fraternity, reactionary old squire.
> He is a do-as-you-would-be-done-by, turn-the-other-cheek kind of person.

INVERTED COMMAS

The use of inverted commas for purposes other than speech can safely be left till later – quotation marks perhaps being regarded as an extension of speech marks. Older pupils should be shown how to use *two* sets of inverted commas, and what to do about other punctuation marks in this case (see pp. 91–2). The stylistic uses of inverted commas, to 'pick out' words for some special reason, can also be discussed with older pupils:

> Slang or figurative language: The teacher allowed himself to be 'needled' by the boy's remarks.

To indicate an ironic or jocular use: The footballer was sent
  off when he expressed some 'opinions' about the referee's
  parentage and eyesight.
To refer to a word itself rather than to its meaning: The
  man painting the sign for 'The Dog and Whistle' forgot
  to leave a space between 'dog' and 'and' and 'and' and
  'whistle'.

Creative punctuation

Punctuation, as has been stressed, is often a way of making
communication more effective, and children should be encouraged to be adventurous in their punctuation, along with
other graphical features.

THIRD-YEAR, MIXED ABILITY

As part of a series of lessons on advertisements, the class have
been asked to cut out advertisements from newspapers and
magazines. In small groups they compare advertisements and
draw up a list of ways in which the advertiser attempts to sell
his product. They then contribute their ideas to a class
discussion – use of colour, attractive/appealing/striking pictures, catchy slogans, humour, extravagant/persuasive language, pseudo-scientific claims, and psychological appeal are
among the topics raised. For homework pupils are asked to
write an advertisement of their own, trying to 'dress-up' an
ordinary product, or sell a product for an unlikely use (honey
as glue is suggested by the teacher). The teacher has a quick
discussion with them on some ways of achieving graphical
emphasis, including underlining, capitalization, different
styles of writing (italics, etc.), exclamation marks, use of
colour, lay-out and spacing.

ELIXIR

Do you sometimes feel tired when you wake up?

DEPRESSED – ANXIOUS – NO ENERGY???

The new miracle wonder-drink

ELIXIR

is the answer.

Scientifically prepared in our laboratories
from a mixture of two parts *hydrogen* and one
part *oxygen* according to a secret process

is Nature's own life-giving drink.

It refreshes!   It revives!!

It gives you that get-up-and-go feeling!!!

ELIXIR means GOOD-BUY to your troubles.

FIFTH-YEAR, 'O' LEVEL GROUP

While commenting on written work which the pupils have
produced, the teacher raises the question of how we can write
something and, at the same time, comment on what we have
written. The class discuss the use of the exclamation mark to
express surprise or draw attention to a particular meaning,
the use of (?) to indicate doubt or reservation, the use of
inverted commas to suggest something is not really meant,
and (*sic*) to express reservations about a quotation. Although
the first two are still sometimes frowned upon in formal
writing, their growing acceptance is an indication that
punctuation is not static and that changes do occur, albeit
gradually.

The principal recommendation of this chapter is that punctuation is best taught to individual pupils as the need for it is

revealed in their written work, and as is appropriate to their developing awareness of, and control over, sentence structure. But it will sometimes be appropriate to summarize and consolidate aspects of punctuation, or to introduce new usages, to the whole class. Such instruction will often arise out of reading and writing which are part of the normal English programme; usually it can be pursued for quite short periods of a lesson, in a fairly lively and enjoyable manner, with active participation by the pupils – 'little but often' might be an apt motto for punctuation teaching. Above all, the attitude to foster is not that 'incorrect' punctuation has to be constantly guarded against but that appropriate punctuation helps to make us more flexible and effective writers.

7

GRAMMAR IN THE CLASSROOM

Teaching 'correct' English

Teaching correct English means teaching the English appropriate to formal written work. This is not solely (or even mainly) a matter of grammar, but also of vocabulary, style and tone, and improvement comes about as the child is exposed to written material through his own reading, and as he undertakes more demanding and varied writing tasks in which his attention is focused on *what* he needs to write about and *how* he can best express himself. That is to say that mastering the grammatical conventions of written English is, for the most part, a by-product of pupils' general linguistic development in the secondary school, and teaching such conventions must go hand in hand with other activities in English.

There is, however, one aspect of 'correct' grammar which English teachers can discuss profitably with their pupils, namely what 'correctness' means. A number of interesting topics arise:

1 What are current attitudes to correct usage? Many usages are disputed – what do the pupils think? Perhaps they could carry out a small survey, using a dozen or so disputed items, of other people's views on correct usage. Are there differences according to age? Are teachers more or less conservative than parents?

2 How have certain usages come to be established as 'correct'? This is a fascinating topic, some aspects of which were touched on in Chapter 4. It will probably surprise pupils to learn that many of our 'incorrect' usages were regarded as perfectly acceptable alternatives in earlier times, and that some became incorrect simply because an individual grammarian decided arbitrarily that they were unacceptable. These 'ipsedixits' ('because I say so') should alert pupils to the lack of logic or rationality underpinning correct usage.

3 What different varieties of English are there? Here pupils might consider not just the different varieties of written English but also varieties of spoken English. They might explore some of the different conventions of American English (for instance, it is quite acceptable to write 'one should never forget his/their cheque card', or to use 'gotten'), or compile lists of slang expressions, or put together a small dialect dictionary. This should help the child to become sensitive to different registers and to realize that, while his own spoken language is nothing to be ashamed of, he needs to widen his linguistic repertoire to become proficient in a variety of language contexts.

Another useful activity is to highlight the differences between speech and writing, and so to underline the need to master different conventions for written language. One way to do this is for pupils, working in pairs, first of all to tape-record an explanation by one to the other (for instance, how to reach school from home, describing an incident or a picture, explaining how to play snakes and ladders), and then to provide a written explanation on the same topic. A number of interesting points should emerge:

(*i*) Since writing provides a permanent record, and does not permit the instantaneous corrections, pauses, and hesitations of speech, it is a deliberate, planned activity in which we need to consider carefully what we put down on paper.

(*ii*) In speech, we are talking to someone, we receive instant feedback from him, and we can use a variety of non-verbal and situational aids to communication. In writing, our addressee is remote, we have no contextual aids, and we must imagine what our reader needs to help him understand our meaning – we must be quite explicit in what we write. So, we tend to draw upon a more sophisticated vocabulary and a more complex and formally correct sentence structure. (The pupils will notice that there are many things on the tape which would not be clear in writing, and some features of the written account which would be unnecessary or sound stilted in speech.)

(*iii*) Because we can usually take our time over writing, we can edit the language, and choose the way in which we express ourselves much more accurately and precisely than is possible in speech. It therefore becomes feasible to stick closely to certain grammatical conventions as well as spelling and punctuation rules. As children move through the secondary school, especially as they undertake varieties of transactional writing (in other subjects as well as English), the teacher may stress the need to edit and redraft the work, proceeding from a rough, general idea of what the pupil wants to say, through amplification, elaboration, selection and arrangement until a satisfying version is arrived at. It is during the redrafting process that grammatical correctness, along with spelling and punctuation, needs to be taken into account. The teacher can wander round the class, giving help to individual pupils. During these 'writing workshops' (or 'writing clinics' as they are sometimes referred to) most of the teacher's comments will no doubt be aimed at content or expression, but there will also be opportunities to pick up inappropriate grammar, not in the sense of rejecting what the pupil has written but of offering him an alternative: 'Can you think of another way of putting that?' 'You might *say* that but do you think you would read it in a book?'

Correcting grammar in pupils' written work needs handling with discretion. Many grammatical errors are just slips, while others are caused by pupil experimentation and trying out complex structures – here the errors are often conceptual in origin. If there is an error of usage (perhaps a persistent one) which the teacher judges should be picked up, it should be pointed out and the pupil encouraged to practise the correct one. As with spelling and punctuation, a workcard and worksheet system may be found useful, provided it is related to individual needs. These points are illustrated in Natalie's essay (pp. 135–6). There are two obvious 'errors' ('the difference between males, females and children', 'when a child has his or her sixteenth birthday they will change') but the first is now, one would judge, acceptable usage, and the second marginal – certainly neither is worth picking up. On the other hand, the awkwardness of 'to tell the difference ... could be shape' and 'they will change according to the sex, they happened to be, their shape' is caused by the child wrestling with difficult concepts and structures, and should be dealt with by discussing the meaning with Natalie.

It is unlikely that sufficient pupils will be making the same kind of error to warrant discussion with the whole class. Where the teacher may touch on grammatical correctness, however, is when setting written tasks in which the question of appropriateness arises, as part of the general programme to extend the pupils' range of writing skills. One tactic is to ask pupils to redraft a passage in more appropriate form. Here, for instance, is a letter to a lost-property office set for a fourth-year CSE group. Pupils discuss what is wrong with it and then re-draft it more appropriately. Content and vocabulary will be the main concerns, but grammatical appropriateness also arises, and the teacher might also wish to reinforce technical points about the lay-out of formal letters.

> Miss J. Smith,
> 23 Lime Close,
> Derby.

Dear man in charge of the lost-property office,

The other day, travelling on one of your buses, my brolly and specs was lost. At least, I hadn't got them when I'd done my shopping, so I guess I must have left them on the bus. Mind you, I could have lost them when I was trying on a new dress. But if either of them have turned up, can you let me know. My granny left the brolly to me when she died, and my mum and me would be very sad if we lost it. It has them old-fashioned twiddly bits round the handle.

Thanking you in anticipation, I remain,
> Yours very obediently,
> Janet Smith.

Another useful exercise is to ask pupils to write in contrasting styles, drawing upon different vocabulary and grammar. For instance, working in threes they could prepare a conversation between father, mother and son or daughter about staying out late at nights. They have to prepare two scenarios, one leading to a heated argument, the other to a reasoned compromise. The scenes can then be acted in front of the class (and tape-recorded) for a discussion of the kind of language used in the two situations, and what it is that helps to produce such different outcomes. Pupils generally find this kind of oral work easier than the corresponding written exercise, but after such a discussion they should be ready to try a similar task in writing. For instance, they might compose letters of complaint to the headmaster on some aspect of school life about which they feel strongly (*i*) in a colloquial, emotive 'I'll say what I think' style and (*ii*) in a more formal, politely-phrased style.

Many of these exercises, which depend on social nuances and sensitivity in personal relationships, can be tried most appropriately with older pupils from the third year upwards. (For other examples, see the 'Language in Use' materials.) There is, however, one context in which secondary school pupils come across varieties of transactional writing from the very beginning, namely in other subjects of the curriculum. In both science and humanities subjects pupils are likely to be asked to carry out formal writing tasks which not only call for standards of correctness in grammar but may also have additional grammatical features peculiar to the subject register. No doubt it is the subject specialist teachers' responsibility to be aware of the language demands of their subjects, and to teach pupils how to cope with them, and English teachers can assist by co-operating with and, if asked, advising other members of staff. Additionally, the English department may find it worthwhile to give some practice in writing various kinds of expository prose, a feature of which will be observing the conventions of formal written English. Some examples might be: take a set of rules for playing a game, or instructions for making up a model kit, or instructions for setting up a tent, and expand them into continuous prose; describe something that happened to you (*i*) in continuous prose, (*ii*) as it might appear in a diary entry; take a set of science notes and write about an experiment (*i*) as if you were explaining it to a friend, (*ii*) in the 'proper' scientific form; describe a road accident (*i*) as a dispassionate bystander, (*ii*) as one (both) of the parties involved, (*iii*) as it might appear in a policeman's notebook, (*iv*) as an account in the local newspaper.

To conclude this section, we cannot do better than quote the words of HMI from the 'Language' section of the working paper 'Curriculum 11–16':

> Pupils aged 11–16 need help in understanding the relevant features of many kinds of language that touch people's lives – their grammars, certainly, but also the reasons for their grammars which lie in the contexts of their use – in the nature and purpose of the task, the nature of the 'audience', the relationship of the speaker and writer with the audience, and the 'match' between language and context.

The above approach is clearly a far cry from teaching 'correct' English through artificial exercises in sentence correction taken completely out of context. The following question occurred on an 'O' level paper some years ago.

> Rewrite the following sentences removing all errors of expression:
> (*a*) Due to his hard work he did as well or even better than expected.
> (*b*) I object to him whistling like he does all day.
> (*c*) Before closing the meeting a vote was taken to decide who they would send.

What is one to make of this kind of exercise? How many of these 'errors' are unequivocally errors and how many are disputed usages? How many are perfectly acceptable colloquialisms? How many are serious errors inasmuch as they either interfere with communication or would be regarded by most people as unpardonable solecisms? After all, the grammar of English *is* changing and usage is only usage. More to the point, training children to correct and explain this kind of 'error' wastes a disproportionate amount of class time and is of little benefit to their own writing.

Some errors, however, may be worth spending a little class time on (perhaps no more than ten- to fifteen-minute sessions) in the upper forms, especially those errors which could cause ambiguity or for which there does seem to be a rational explanation. Chief among these is the 'wrong reference' error – where there is confusion over the noun or verb to which a qualifier refers. Most notorious is the 'misrelated participle' which is best not regarded as an error *sui generis* unless there is potential confusion. The effects can be quite humorous and pupils might have fun composing their own examples. Perhaps they can try to cram as many deliberate errors as possible into a short passage:

A Walk in the Country

Unaccustomed to country life, the cock woke us on our first morning, and we decided to go for a walk before breakfast. Opening the back door, the sun shone brightly on our faces. We crossed the farmyard where, grunting and squealing loudly, the farmer was driving his pigs into the van ready to set off for market. We came across a dead fox walking over the fields. Coming upon a fast-flowing river, it proved impassable to the intrepid travellers swollen by the rain of the previous night. . . .

A general rule of proximity can be applied – a participle phrase will normally be taken as referring to the noun closest to it. The same 'rule' can be applied to clauses and prepositional phrases:

The thief left the car outside a police-station which was later found abandoned. I saw a man talking to a policeman who looked like the owner.

And pupils may enjoy making up advertisements along the lines of: 'Second-hand car wanted by retired vicar in good condition.' Sometimes there can be genuine ambiguity about the meaning, and pupils might be invited to give both possible meanings of:

I watched the stranger from across the road.
This is a photo of the bike which I took on holiday.

The placing of adverbs is especially critical and major differences of meaning can be caused by shifts of position. Try the different placings of 'even' in the sentence 'He was not upset by your insults'.

> Even he (hot-tempered as he is) was not upset by your insults.
> He was not even upset (let alone severely offended) by your insults.
> He was not upset even by your insults (rude though they were).
> He was not upset by even your insults (although you are his friend).

Pupils might see how many meanings they can obtain from inserting 'only' in 'He eats school dinner on Thursdays' or speculate on the unlikely circumstances of 'The kitchen needs painting badly'.

A closely related type of error is confusion over the reference of pronouns. Again, these can be merely amusing:

> Every time he opens his mouth he puts his foot in it.
> Don't kill your wife. Let us do it for you. (Notice outside laundry.)
> When the burglar carrying the stolen cup saw the policeman, he lost his head and it rolled onto the floor.

But there can be real ambiguity. Can the pupils find the four different meanings, according to whom the two 'he's' refer to, of 'The headmaster told the boy that he didn't know what he was talking about'? A special case of ambiguity arises because the -self pronouns function as both reflexive and emphatic:

> Teacher requires self-contained flat where she can cook herself.
> I understand the arguments of the pro-hunting lobby, for I have hunted and shot myself.

The errors so far discussed are primarily matters of clumsy

or confusing expression. There is another type of error where there may be no possible ambiguity and yet there is fairly widespread agreement that the grammar is incorrect in written English. In such cases it is always a matter of judgement as to how far there *is* a general consensus on the appropriate usage – but where it does exist it seems worthwhile to point out the usage to older pupils.

Chief among these are errors of agreement, where the number, person or tense in one part of a sentence does not agree with that in another part:

> The price of potatoes have risen.
> The King, flanked by the choicest of his knights, were visible on the battlefield.
> Because the dog is the friendliest of pets, they are often known as man's best friend.
> The dark stranger strode into the saloon, draws out his gun, and shoots the sheriff dead.

The important thing is consistency. Some words can be singular or plural, but not both in the same sentence:

> The visiting team has already taken the field and are practising shooting-in.
> When a council makes a compulsory purchase order, they do not have to give detailed reasons.

This kind of error occurs from time to time in pupils' writing, and can be usefully discussed with individual pupils.

More dubious are the 'rules' of agreement after certain allegedly singular words like no one, either, neither, each, and the rule for consistency after the indefinite pronoun 'one'. 'One can only do his best, even if they fail' would, I suppose, be felt to be incorrect by most educated writers but what about 'One may not like his arguments, but you have to admire his persistence'? And the following usages seem nowadays to be on the fringes of acceptability:

> Neither hockey nor football are popular at our school.

Each of the children have their own library books. (Is 'his' sexist and 'his or her' clumsy?)

Even more dubious are the rules for cases in English pronouns. Case is largely redundant in English so that, except in clearly unambiguous positions, it appears to be weakening, especially after prepositions and the who/whom distinction. There is a clear rule-of-thumb which helps to indicate the correct case when a noun and pronoun are used together – try the pronoun on its own.

(*a*) My brother and me are going to the match. (Me am going to the match?

(*b*) He left a message for my sister and I. (He left a message for I?)

Because of the opprobrium attached to the 'me' usage in (*a*), 'I' is somehow felt to be more 'proper', so we get falsely analogous over-corrections like (*b*), or 'between you and I' or the notice which appeared on the staff notice board 'The latest wage offer is an insult to we teachers'. But the very fact that one has to stop and work out the correct usage indicates that one is dealing with a marginal and probably no longer tenable distinction.

One type of error which may be worth some attention with older pupils is 'unequal yoking', the linking together of grammatical units which do not really belong together. How serious this is is again a matter of judgement: I admit to not noticing or being disturbed by 'The grass was cut and the seeds planted' or 'He likes to play football in the winter and swimming in the summer', but to being put out by 'He is as tall if not taller than his father' and 'He is deeply interested and fascinated by butterflies'. In these latter cases, a construction one expects to be completed is not completed, and communication is momentarily impaired. Likewise, I would regard as a harmless and comprehensible contraction 'Like cricket, the laws of rugby are complicated', but would feel that the syntax of this sentence had gone wrong at the planning stage:

> The Prime Minister, a man of considerable obstinacy, and who has made his views quite clear on this subject, refused to withdraw his remarks.

It may be inferred, then, that it is partly a matter for the individual teacher to judge what conventions to bring to the notice of pupils, and how much time to spend on them. The suggestions in the preceding paragraphs will probably have upset as many readers by what they include as by what they omit. It is important to give pupils some guidance as to the most widely accepted conventions of written usage, but not to fight unnecessary battles and not to get involved in lengthy pseudo-grammatical explanations. Here, to complete the reader's disillusionment, is a list of some of the commonly-presented 'correct' usages which I personally would not want to bother with, both because the status of the usage itself is controversial and because, in most cases, there is no justification (historical or grammatical) for it.

different from (to, than)   in (under) the circumstances
try to (and)   less/fewer   due to/owing to
very/quite unique   we are much (very) amused
who/whom   it is I (me)   hold tight(ly)   come quick(ly)
shall/will (in most cases interchangeable)
not ending a sentence with a preposition
not splitting infinitives
than cannot be a preposition (who says so?) — He is taller than I (me).
the fused participle — I don't like your (you) lying to me.
superlative for comparative — John and David did their best, but David was the fastest.

Using grammatical terms: literature teaching

The aim here is not primarily to teach grammatical

nomenclature for its own sake, but to use grammatical terms for other purposes during the English lesson and to teach only incidentally the meaning of these terms. In literature lessons, the teacher may find it helpful to use grammatical terms when discussing a writer's work and how he achieves his effects. For instance, if a second year class are looking at D.H. Lawrence's 'Kangaroo', it might be convenient to refer to the poet's use of adjectives.

> Delicate mother kangaroo
> Sitting up there rabbit-wise, but huge, plump-weighted,
> And lifting her beautiful slender face, oh! so much
>   more gently and finely-lined than a rabbit's or than a
>   hare's,
> Lifting her face to nibble at a round white peppermint drop
>   which she loves, sensitive mother Kangaroo.
>
> Her sensitive, long, pure-bred face.
> Her full antipodal eyes, so dark,
> So big and quiet and remote, having watched so many
>   empty dawns in silent Australia.
> Her little loose hands, and drooping Victorian shoulders,
> And then her great weight below the waist, her vast pale
>   belly
> With a thin young yellow little paw hanging out, and
>   straggle of a long thin ear, like ribbon,
> Like a furry trimming in the middle of her belly, thin
>   little dangle of an immature paw, and one thin ear.

Clearly, a discussion of the poem might take many forms, but at some stage a teacher might want to direct the children's attention to descriptions of the kangaroo's face ('slender', 'gently and finely-lined', 'sensitive, long, pure-bred'), her eyes ('full, dark, big, quiet, remote' and so to get at 'antipodal'), or her baby ('thin young yellow little paw ... straggle of a long thin ear'), and to use 'adjectives' as a convenient term in this discussion.

Or, if a fourth-year class are beginning *Great Expectations*, the teacher might wish to look more closely at this passage:

> A fearful man, all in coarse grey, with a great iron on his leg. A man with no hat, and with broken shoes, and with an old rag tied round his head. A man who had been soaked in water, and smothered in mud, and lamed by stones, and cut by flints, and stung by nettles, and torn by briars; who limped and shivered and glared and growled; and whose teeth chattered in his head as he seized me by the chin.

Here the teacher might want to ask the class what impression the convict makes on them, and to bring out the tension between the fear he inspires in Pip and the pity Dickens none the less manages to arouse in the reader. This is best done by directing attention to the *verbs* of the passage: the contrast between 'limped/shivered' and 'glared/growled', between 'chattered' and 'seized'; the way in which nature seems to be 'ganging-up' on the convict – 'soaked in water, smothered in mud...'. (With an 'A' level group one might want to highlight the characteristic energy of the writing, achieved here by the peculiar syntax.)

At a more sophisticated level, with an 'O' or 'A' level class, one might look at the sentence structure of a writer such as Lawrence.

> There was no noise anywhere. Evidently the children had not been wakened, or had gone to sleep again. A train, three miles away, roared across the valley. The night was very large, and very strange, stretching its hoary distances infinitely. And out of the silver grey fog of darkness came sounds vague and hoarse: a corncrake not far off, sound of a train like a sigh, and distant shouts of men.

> Her quietened heart beginning to beat quickly again, she hurried down the side garden to the back of the house. Softly she lifted the latch; the door was still bolted, shut hard against her.

> (D. H. Lawrence, *Sons and Lovers*, Chapter 1)

Again, there are many things one might want to say about this passage, but the syntax deserves particular attention. There is not a single subordinate clause in the extract, and yet there is remarkable and effective variety. One might especially look at the alternation of short and long sentences, the almost poetic rhythm of the writing, and the inversion of normal word order to achieve particular effects. (What difference would it make if Lawrence had written 'Vague and hoarse sounds came out of the darkness' or 'She lifted the latch softly'?)

We should make it clear that we are not advocating 'using' literature as the basis of grammar lessons. For instance, one course book misses out the adjectives and adverbs from a passage by Dickens and asks 'What words do the adjectives and adverbs tell us about? What is the function of the adjectives and adverbs?' This is a travesty of English teaching. If a teacher does *not* find it helpful to use 'adjective' and 'adverb' in the normal course of his English lessons, there is no reason why he should feel obliged to do so.

Using grammatical terms: pupils' writing

The most frequent use for grammatical terminology will be in connection with pupils' written work – indeed, we have seen in earlier chapters instances where grammatical terms were helpful in explaining points of spelling or punctuation. It is important, however, to be quite clear about objectives: we do not seek to improve pupils' work by teaching grammar, nor to use pupils' written work in order to teach grammar; the over-riding concern is to help pupils write and, as an aid to this, grammatical terminology may help to focus and highlight certain features of their writing. We make no great claims for grammar here – again, if a teacher does not find the terminology helpful he need have no compunction about avoiding it. In addition, the teacher must judge whether a whole class would benefit from this kind of focusing, or whether he would do best to provide this help for individual children during his writing workshops. Below are three examples of class lessons where the teacher judged that grammatical focusing would be appropriate.

FIRST-YEAR, MIXED ABILITY

Individual children volunteer to mime the movement of particular characters given to them by the teacher. The class have to guess who the character is (a proud lady, a drunken man, a fashion-conscious girl in high heels and tight skirt, a blind man – and so on). The class try to describe the movements as accurately as possible, and the teacher builds up on the board two columns – verbs and adverbs – of words suggested by the children (strut, stagger, totter, stumble – haughtily, daintily, etc.). The children are then asked to give an account of a walk in the town centre on a busy shopping day, and four people whom they see there. They must plan first who the four people are, and how they move, so as to write at least two sentences about each. The teacher stresses that, in marking the children's work, he will be looking especially for the verbs and adverbs used to describe the movement of their characters.

SECOND-YEAR, MIXED ABILITY

The teacher has brought in and placed on the wall a large picture of a ramshackle, broken-down barn. He discusses with them, for about five minutes, what sort of building it is, why they think it might have got into that state, what details they can see in the picture which suggest it is now abandoned. He then asks them to imagine a house that has been deserted for some time. Gingerly, they push the door and it slowly opens. They are to shut their eyes and imagine what it is like. What are the first things that strike them? What does it smell like? They stand very quiet inside the house. What can they hear? When they open their eyes, what do they see? On the board the teacher collects the children's suggestions, looking especially for adjectives and participles (musty, stale, damp, clammy — creaking, scuttling, peeling, and so on). The children plan a description 'The Deserted House' to be written up for homework. The teacher says he is going to judge their work by the quality of the descriptive writing — how well they conjure up the smells, sounds and sights of the building. Just before the end of the lesson he reads 'Mariana' by Tennyson, and the class comment on some of the adjectives used in this poem.

THIRD-YEAR, TOP BAND

Five children have arranged with the teacher to talk to a small group about some hobby or activity they know a lot about, and to bring in any equipment to help them with their talk. For example, one boy talks about how to play snooker (equipped with cue and set of balls), and a girl explains how to crochet. The talks last for about fifteen minutes and are tape-recorded. After the talk, both the original speaker and his hearers try to write down instructions on 'How to play snooker', 'How to crochet', etc. In a later lesson, the teacher selects bits from two of the tape-recordings to compare with the written instructions and the class discuss the differences between them, the teacher noting some of the main findings on the board. They are struck by how much is implicit in the talks because of the availability of context clues, both of the practical 'showing how it's done' kind, and feed-back and questioning from the listeners; in contrast the need to be explicit in writing is obvious from some of the less successful attempts. They notice the use of conjunctions, especially to indicate sequence (after, then, when), and the more complete and formal sentence structure compared with the broken sentences of speech. The teacher has spent a lot of time vetting the tape-recordings and selecting written accounts for comparison, and his reward is the lively interest shown by the pupils. (Some of them ask to hear the tape-recordings *not* played back in the lesson.)

Using grammatical terms: improving sentence structure

In all the illustrations just presented the use of grammatical terminology has been incidental to the lesson, an aid to the teacher and pupils in focusing on certain aspects of their written work. It is sometimes suggested that more systematic grammatical work can be helpful in giving pupils practice in handling a range of structural possibilities. It used to be fashionable to advocate 'graded' English courses, whereby pupils started by practising simple sentences and worked their way up through increasingly complex sentence patterns. The claim was that such practice gave pupils confidence in handling a variety of sentence types in their own writing. As we saw in Chapter 4, this claim is certainly unfounded, at least as far as any overt grammatical component is concerned. The *practice* may have been useful, but this throws the onus back on the teacher to judge what kinds of writing experience will best promote development. The central question is whether grammatically-based practice is of any benefit divorced from contexts in which children genuinely have something worthwhile to write about.

As far as secondary school pupils are concerned, the exercises likely to be most useful are those relating to syntactic development – attention to sentence structure in various ways:

(*a*) Avoiding run-on sentences. This is quite a common 'fault' in the writing of first- and second-year pupils. Attention to this can be linked to punctuation work on the sentence, and to the use of conjunctions and other connecting devices to join sentences. (See Chapter 6, p. 85).

(*b*) Avoiding excessive use of a limited number of co-ordinating conjunctions ('and', 'then', 'so' are the favourites). Again, at a certain stage of their writing development, children are very prone to this, and the objective would be to get them to practise a wider range of connectives.

(c) Using subordinating conjunctions to turn simple into complex sentences. The exercise might take the form of joining sentences in different ways, rearranging sentences, or using more appropriate joining words.

(d) Using varied sentence structures. The pupils practise various types of sentence – simple, multiple, complex and compound. (See, for instance, the game 'Sentence Power' reported in *English in Education*, 8.3.1974.) This kind of exercise is most useful if it can be linked to particular effects in the child's writing, or effects noticed in books being read in class. For instance, one might discuss the use of different-length sentences – short sentences as the climax of an exciting story is reached, longer sentences in more reflective or descriptive passages.

(e) Variations of word order. We have already noted how changes in word order can alter the meaning of sentences.

On Sunday, I promised to return the book you lent me.
I promised to return on Sunday the book you lent me.
I promised to return the book on (about) Sunday you lent me.
I promised to return the book you lent me on Sunday.

More interesting, perhaps, is the use of unusual word order for particular effects, the 'foregrounding' techniques used by authors for emphasis.

Down to the River Weser the Pied Piper led them. Save for one plump rat, drowned were they all. Alone he survived, and lonely he remains.

Clearly, there is a problem of timing here. Whereas (a) and (b) might be appropriate exercises for some first-year pupils, (e) might be worth discussing only with a few fourth- or fifth-year pupils. And since children develop at different rates, it is unlikely that a particular exercise will be appropriate for a whole class. Syntactic help will be most effective when linked to children's own writing. For instance, a teacher may find a child using rather monotonous simple or multiple sentences. He discusses with the child how to make the sentences more varied, and gives him a worksheet with some practice examples. It is, however, important that the teacher keeps an eye on the next few pieces of work and perhaps reminds the pupil; if there is no transfer from the exercises then they are not worth doing.

There is one further drawback to the use of artificial exercises of this kind. Since they tend to concentrate on one kind of structure, they may actually be counter-productive by *limiting* the pupils' response. For instance, one exercise gives a list of subordinating conjunctions and asks pupils to use them to join pairs of sentences.

> Join these sentences in 3 different ways:
> We pitched our tent. The grass was dry.

Presumably what is wanted is something like 'We pitched our tent when/where/because the grass was dry'. But aside from inviting the slightly odd responses 'We pitched our tent if/although the grass was dry', this exercise also closes down the opportunities for children to employ a variety of embedding structures. A mature writer would quite likely write the far less cumbersome 'We pitched our tent on the dry grass'. The trouble with concoctions like 'We went to the shops which were nearby in order that we might purchase provisions before we went on holiday' is that they discourage children from writing 'before going on holiday we went to our local shops to buy provisions'.

Using grammatical terms: teaching cohesion

As pupils move into the upper forms of secondary schools, the focus of attention shifts from the syntax of sentences to the structure of paragraphs or even whole essays. What matters is the total effectiveness of a piece of writing which, at the structural level, often means the way in which the sense is carried through from one sentence to the next, the way a paragraph is constructed, the way sentences and paragraphs are counter-balanced, the way the writer's argument develops through the structure of an essay. The way in which a piece of writing 'hangs together' is called 'cohesion'. The three extracts from essays which follow are by third-year pupils and illustrate different levels of skill in the management of cohesion. The teacher has asked them to write about what it would be like to live in a two-dimensional world, having briefly discussed with them some of the activities which would prove difficult in such a world.

> The people who live in this world are flat, everything is flat.
>
> The people move around like an elastic band, they can stretch as far as they want to.
>
> Trees are grown in this land not up vertical but trees are grown horizontally along the ground. All their food is grown like this.
>
> These people don't drink water, they drink juices out of the leaves on the trees.
>
> The people haven't got any housing, so they live on the land.
>
> To reproduce they do it exactly the same way as Human Beings.
>
> Even though the world is flat air can still move around.
>
> Sometimes when they were sleeping on the ground they would find little holes in the ground and sleep in these cracks.
>
> (*Louise*)

The creatures are covered in a slimy film. When they want

to move along they jolt their body and slide on their slippery surface. Their eyes are embedded in the sides of the creatures (which is one molecule high) which enables them to see other creatures coming. If there is another creature straight in front they would slide to the side because they can't get over each other because there is no height. They have no houses because there is no height. There is no rain, and light or any other weather so they cannot get cold and have no need of them. They can see in the dark with their highly sensitive eyes and their 'skin' is slightly fluorescent so they can see each other easily. They have very sensitive skins and if they touch each other they will break up and decompose. They can sense if anybody else is coming by nerves on the bottom of their body which can feel the slight vibration caused by another creature. . . .

(Stephen)

Living in a world of two dimensions would obviously create a great deal of problems for us, as there is no up or down or height. For example moving, eating, recognition and reproducing. Anyone living in a world such as this would naturally have to be flat, like a piece of paper. Some could live on water like flat waterboatmen with hair like the paramecium with cilia. These people would have the cilia with front oars and legs but would be the shape of a male or female. The legs and oars would slide along the water shooting them along and the hairs would help this movement.

To tell the difference between males, females and children could be shape. For example, males could be shaped as squares, females could be shaped as triangles and children under the age of fifteen would have circulars as their shape. This means that when a child has his or her sixteenth birthday then they will change according to the sex, they happened to be, their shape. Although this solves a sex problem and age problem, there is still the problem of

nationality. This could be solved by having one part of the
body with the flag on it. Another way is to be the colour of
the part of the world you come from. . . .

(*Natalie*)

Clearly, one might comment on this work at many levels.
(In terms of the amount written, Louise's essay is complete
except for a diagram and two sentences, about half of
Stephen's essay is quoted, and a quarter of Natalie's, exclud-
ing three diagrams.) One is struck by the simplicity and
directness of Louise's account, the imaginativeness and rich-
ness of scientific vocabulary in Stephen's, and the rather literal
approach of Natalie's with its failure really to envisage the
problems of a two-dimensional world. However, at the level
of cohesion there are striking developmental differences.
Louise makes little attempt at cohesion. Almost every
sentence is a separate idea, signalled by the very short
paragraphs. The effect is of a list of almost disconnected
statements. Stephen's main connecting device is the subordinating conjunction; indeed, he has reached the stage, fairly
common in second- and third-year pupils, of 'over-subordina-
tion', and this leads him into a rather repetitive clumsiness.
One or two other cohesive devices are used, but not convinc-
ingly. (In '. . . they have no need of them', the reference of
'them' is not immediately apparent.) Whatever one may think
of the content of Natalie's essay, there is no doubt she shows
the greatest mastery of cohesion, employing an impressive
range of cohesive strategies, so that the reader is carried along
on the tide of the discussion. Some of the major cohesive
devices are:

(*i*) continual reference back to what has gone before,
through the use of repetition, pronouns, demonstra-
tives, comparison, etc. ('a world such as this', 'these
people would have the cilia', 'this means that', 'this
could be solved by', repetition of 'cilia', 'oars', 'legs',
'hairs').

(*ii*) the omission of words and phrases that can be understood by what has already been written (e.g. 'some could live' compared with the repetition of 'the people' and 'trees' in Louise's). This is the obverse of (*i*), and this continual cross-referencing engages the reader in the text and forces him to grapple with its meaning.

(*iii*) the use of conjunctions (especially 'logical' ones) and sentence adverbs to stress logical relationships within the text ('although', 'naturally', 'for example', 'another way'). These serve to underline a writer's thread of argument – indeed, they often serve as 'pegs' on which a writer can hang his developing theme.

There are many other cohesive devices, not all of them grammatical (for instance, semantic relations between words) and, at the inter-paragraph level, we are also dealing with large-scale contrasts, comparisons, parallelisms, analogies, examples, and so on. Again, we are not suggesting that the teacher undertake formal instruction in cohesion, using a host of technical terms, but that he might make pupils (from the third year onwards) aware of some of the possibilities, in order to make their own writing more cohesive. The following ideas may prove useful in teaching cohesion:

(*a*) Simply to illustrate what cohesion means, cloze procedure can be used. This involves presenting a passage, but missing out words at regular intervals (say, every five or seven words) and asking the class to guess them. This demonstrates that reading means both referring back to what has gone before and scanning ahead, making use of what one might call the 'cohesive redundancy' of most written texts. (Of course a teacher may cheat in the words he omits so as to make the point about cohesion clearer.)

(*b*) The pupils can redraft pieces of writing in which the cohesion is poor. They could work on redrafting an essay in pairs or small groups, and be prepared to justify their alterations in ensuing class discussion.

(c) When helping individual pupils with their written work, the teacher can show them how to use 'logical' connectives to improve the effectiveness of their writing. Indeed, with a fourth-year class, working on argumentative or discursive writing, it might be appropriate to draw up a list of some of these connectives – however, on the other hand, moreover, in addition, therefore, indeed, it follows that, firstly ... secondly, furthermore – the list can be extended as the pupils bring forward more and more examples.

(d) At some time during the later years of secondary school, most pupils will need some help with the structuring of paragraphs. Over a period they could be introduced to some of the major kinds of paragraph organization: the series of statements leading to a conclusion; the general statement illustrated by examples; the paragraph with two balanced or contrasting halves. (For a fuller discussion of paragraph types see J. Gilliland in the appendix.) Occasionally pupils might be given some basic material and asked to write differently structured paragraphs using it, as in the following example written around 'The policeman's lot is not a happy one!'.

> Imagine yourself faced by a seething mass of football supporters chanting abuse and hurling missiles at you. You move into the crowd to stop an ugly fight which is developing. The crowd closes against you. Someone knocks off your helmet. You are punched, battered and bruised. If you arrest someone the cry of 'fascist pig' goes up. The policeman's lot is not a happy one.

> The policeman's lot is not a happy one. He may be called upon to intervene in a drunken brawl, interview a distraught old lady whose purse has been snatched, run the half-suppressed gauntlet of sneering comments. And after hours pounding the beat he returns to the station only to face complaints because he has fallen behind with filling in his reports.

> Among a policeman's many duties are the maintenance of

law and order, often in the most trying circumstances, presenting evidence in court, completing interminable reports, in fact acting as general dogsbody. It may seem as though the policeman's lot is not a happy one. Yet it has its compensations too – the gratitude of the old lady whose purse has been returned to her, the overwhelming relief of the parents whose lost child has been found, the quiet word which keeps a youngster out of trouble – these are the rewards of the job.

(*e*) On an even grander scale, some attention should be paid to the over-all structure of a piece of writing at the planning stage. Pupils need to think about the development of the argument from paragraph to paragraph, and some thought might be given to the way in which paragraphs could be linked and how the topic is to be introduced and concluded. Although the use of literary 'models' is generally frowned upon, the occasional use of a model to provide the cohesive structure of a piece of writing can be helpful.

FOURTH-YEAR, 'O' LEVEL GROUP

The teacher read with the class James Thurber's short story 'The Night the Ghost Got In', and they discussed how Thurber achieved his humorous effects. They then analysed the structure of the story, and the teacher wrote an outline on the blackboard:

Par. 1 Bald statement and summary: 'The ghost that got into our house...'

Par. 2 Description of the strange phenomena: 'They began about a quarter past one...'

Pars. 3–5 Involvement of the rest of the family and neighbours.

Pars. 6–12 Involvement of the police: 'The police were on hand in a commendably short time...'

Par. 13 The punch line.

The pupils were then asked, for homework, to write their own short story, following the same general plan: statement of incredible event; description; complication; resolution; punch-line – and some lively accounts were produced along the lines of 'The Night We Had a Tiger in our Bathroom'.

Clearly, the kind of work we are advocating is very different from the 'insert suitable adjectives in the following sentences' or 'give the collective noun for peacocks' type of exercise. And this is deliberately so. The foregoing pages are not essentially about teaching grammar at all, but about using grammar to help children with their written work. This draws upon the teacher's grammatical knowledge, not the pupil's. It does not really matter, for instance, whether the pupil knows the term 'sentence adverbs' provided he understands their use in his own writing – and for this purpose knowing the term may focus attention and facilitate discussion.

Exploring the grammar of the mother tongue

Helping children to examine objectively the way their own language works can be, for older pupils, an exciting activity, having something of the quality of genuine scientific enquiry. Indeed, 'teaching' is perhaps a misnomer here, since the teacher needs to abandon any kind of didactic role and become a co-researcher alongside the pupil. He may suggest fruitful areas for enquiry, he may provide language samples, he may indicate useful analytic techniques, but he will not *tell* the pupils what the 'rules' are, nor set them futile exercises in applying the rules. If this kind of enquiry is to have any value it must be substantially carried out by the pupils themselves. We give two examples of the method of controlled induction applied to grammar teaching.

THIRD-YEAR, TOP SET

The lesson started from the curious fact that, although the children could readily explain the common structures for asking a question in French, they were unable to give the corresponding 'rules' for asking a question in their own mother tongue – this despite the fact that they were much more confident questioners in English than in French. Did we have similar rules in English? The teacher suggested that each child write down and bring to a future lesson a number of different kinds of question.

At the beginning of the lesson the teacher collected examples from the children and wrote them on the board, asking them if they could see and describe any common patterns. The teacher suggested the technique of comparing questions with the corresponding statements. The pupils quickly found the following patterns:

(*i*) Auxiliary verb – Subject – Main verb (Can I have a piece of cake?)
(*ii*) Does/did – Subject – Main verb (Do you know the answer? Did he do it?). Why do we need to 'invent' an auxiliary verb?
(*iii*) Main verb – Subject (Is he clever?)
(*iv*) Use of question markers – Why, when, how, where, etc. These were listed.

The pupils now tried to formulate the rules they had discovered, and one or two sentences were discussed which seemed to require modifications to the rules. (Which book did he borrow? Has he got the money?)

(For a fuller discussion of this lesson and its rationale see 'The excitement of grammar', *Use of English*, 21.3.1970.)

SIXTH-FORM, GENERAL STUDIES

As part of a series of lessons on language use the class had been considering the meaning of 'meaning', and the teacher raised the question of whether the grammar of a language 'meant' anything. He wrote on the board the well-known first verse of 'Jabberwocky':

> 'Twas brillig, and the slithy toves
> Did gyre and gimble in the wabe;
> All mimsy were the borogoves
> And the mome raths outgrabe.

He asked them what clues there were to the meanings of the 'nonsense' words – how they knew what sorts of words they were. In the ensuing discussion the following points emerged:

(*i*) some words served mainly to 'signal' a particular part of speech – 'twas, the, did.

(*ii*) some words served mainly to signal relationships between other words – and, in.

(*iii*) some inflexions carried a kind of meaning and also signalled parts of speech – -s ending for plurals, 'outgrabe' almost certainly a verb in the past tense.

The teacher pointed out that, taking all these together, we could construct sentence patterns which had little semantic meaning and yet 'meant' a great deal.

The _____ _____s did _____ and _____ in the _____.
The _____s were all _____ and the _____ _____s _____ed.

The pupils were asked what parts of speech should go in each of these gaps and were invited to construct their own sentences, as bizarre or vivid as possible!

These two lessons illustrate some of the major features of English grammar and some useful techniques of grammatical analysis:

(*a*) There is a small number of basic sentence patterns in English, whose word-order carries the main grammatical meaning.

(*b*) The main content words (words which have high semantic meaning) can be divided into four classes or parts of speech (traditionally called noun, verb, adjective and adverb) according to their function. Function depends on position in the sentence and cannot always be derived from the meaning of the word. These four classes can be explored by the technique of substitution in basic sentence patterns, and by the use of 'nonsense' words to filter off the semantic meaning. The basic word classes can be expanded into phrases and clauses.

(*c*) There is a small number of very common function and structure words which have negligible or low semantic meaning but which serve to signal or 'mark' grammatical relationships. Some examples are: noun markers (a, the), verb markers (is, do, have), phrase markers (in, of, by), clause markers (because, if, so), connectives (and, but), question markers (when, why, how), intensifiers (very, quite).

(*d*) Morphological changes (inflection) also signal a few grammatical relationships in English, but far fewer than in highly inflected languages like Latin or Old English. The main ones are inflections for plurals, tenses and participles, case in pronouns (and the 's in nouns), comparative and superlative endings. There are also morphological features which strongly suggest the word class, for instance, -ness usually indicates a noun and -ly an adverb (but not always – 'lowly', 'kindly').

These four linguistic features are described and categorized differently in different grammars. The teacher who wishes to try out this kind of grammatical enquiry should keep the terminology simple and not insist on imposing a particular terminology and categorization on the pupils.

One or two other techniques for examining grammatical structure may briefly be mentioned.

(*a*) The dependence of a word on function rather than meaning for determining its class can be illustrated by the use of nonsense words in basic sentence patterns. Consider, for instance, the following sentences:

1 The grimbles gambol gleefully on the green grass.
2 The goats grimble gleefully on the green grass.

3 The goats gambol grimbly on the green grass.
4 The goats gambol gleefully on the grimble grass.

What part of speech is 'grimble' in each of these sentences? How do you know? Can you turn 1 and 2 into the singular and the past tense? Can you turn 3 and 4 into the comparative and superlative? After playing around with these sentences, pupils might be asked to use 'round' and 'down' in as many distinct grammatical ways as they can, including both parts of speech and function/structure words.

(*b*) Expansion games. These can be quite fun for exploring the ways in which a sentence can be elaborated. For instance, pupils could expand the nominal group along the lines of 'the great, grey-green, greasy Limpopo'. Taking it in turns they could build up a series like 'Jim has a large nose ... a large red nose ... a large red ugly nose...', or each addition may be more complex than the previous one: 'a large nose ... a large wart-covered nose ... a large wart-covered nose with purple spots ... a large wart-covered nose with purple spots which is always running...' A variant on this is to use a basic substitution frame, with the children, competing in teams, completing it alphabetically:

My uncle Algernon has an awful armadillo which acts atrociously.
My aunt Beatrice has a brown bear which bulges badly.

X and Z are best omitted, but we might be able to cope with:

My uncle Quentin has a quarrelsome quagga which quacks querulously.

(*c*) Word-order and meaning. The importance of word-order in English is readily illustrated by sentences where changes in the word-order alter the functions of words and change the meaning. We have already considered the sentences:

On Sunday I promised to return the book you lent me.
I promised to return on Sunday the book you lent me.

> I promised to return the book on Sunday which you lent
> me.
> I promised to return the book you lent me on Sunday.

What is the function of 'on Sunday' in each of these sentences, and what part of speech is it substituting for?

> If we travel hopefully, we should complete the journey
> safely.
> If we travel, hopefully we shall complete the journey safely.

This makes an interesting pair for discussion, not only because of the differing functions of 'hopefully', but also because it illustrates the way in which English grammar is continually changing. (I say this hopefully; hopefully no one is going to object to this useful colloquialism.) A particularly telling way of making the point about word-order is to ask the pupils to talk for a few minutes in small groups, deliberately trying to alter one of the main syntactic rules. For instance one could insist that the verb always preceded the subject, or adjectives always followed nouns, or the sentence pattern should be object—verb—subject. A few minutes is all the pupils will manage; not only is the language barely comprehensible, even when the rules are known, but the effort of talking is a great strain on the speakers.

(*d*) Grammar and style. Pupils may be encouraged to examine the grammar of actual samples of written language material. For instance, as part of a study of the press they could, working in groups, compare similar items (sports pages, news stories) in different newspapers. This work would be inductive – they should be encouraged to make hypotheses about the language (e.g. sentence length, sentence complexity, use of adjectives) and then to check these hypotheses against the data. They could then speculate on the reasons for the differences in style. Do different styles make different demands on the reader? Does this suggest anything about the potential readership? Does the style match other features of the newspapers – their lay-out, illustrations, political slant, choice of vocabulary?

Another example of this kind of work is the lesson already discussed in which pupils compare spoken with written explanations. As part of this, they might comment on some major grammatical differences between spoken and written English. It is important for pupils to realize that grammar varies according to medium, context, and purpose – that different registers employ grammars which differ to a greater or lesser extent.

(*e*) Comparison of different grammatical systems. It often comes as a surprise to pupils to realize that they have a much greater objective knowledge of the grammar of a foreign language which they are learning than of their own mother tongue, which they handle intuitively in a much more idiomatic fashion. It is worth discussing this paradox and what it means to 'know' the grammar of a language. Comparisons with the grammar of a foreign language are illuminating: what are the main grammatical differences between English and French – for a start, what do they find odd or difficult about French grammar (gender and agreement, irregular verbs [do we have them in English?], the subjunctive mood)? If there is a non-native English speaker in the class, or if one is willing to come in to talk to them, he could discuss the problems he had learning English and what features he finds difficult. It is salutary to see one's language through the eyes of a non-native speaker. If the teacher knows anyone who has a knowledge of a non-Indo-European language, such a language usually presents quite different grammatical structures and provides a striking contrast with English. Finally, pupils may find it interesting to look back in time and see how English grammar has changed over the centuries. A short passage from Old English, for instance, shows that while we can recognize and understand the meaning of many of the words used, the grammar has changed out of all recognition. A comparison of *Sir Gawain and the Green Knight* with extracts from Shakespeare shows how, in a relatively short space of time, an unfamiliar grammar became very much the grammar which we still use today. A discussion of why this happened provides interesting insights into the social history of the period. In this historical context, pupils can look at the way grammar is changing today and, perhaps, some of the linguistic relics of the past (for instance, 's to show the possessive).

The examples of grammar teaching given so far are concerned mainly with an inductive study of the surface features of grammar, that is with structural grammar of some kind. To explain the hierarchical organization of grammar, how the surface features relate to the underlying knowledge of grammar – that intuitive competence which all native speakers possess – we must turn to transformational-generative grammar. What matters here are not the particular analytic systems employed by transformational grammarians, but the central concept that grammar is not fully explicable in terms of surface features and especially that grammar is not separable from semantic meaning – that to understand fully how grammar works we must infer the native speaker's semantic knowledge.

This latter point is best illustrated by asking pupils to consider ambiguous or potentially ambiguous statements. The sentence 'It's too hot to eat' has three possible meanings depending partly on the semantic meaning of 'hot' and partly on the reference of 'it'.

The cat is too hot to eat.
The weather is too hot to eat.
The food is too hot (spicy or scalding) to eat.

These three sentences are, on the surface, grammatically identical, but we must suppose the speaker knows intuitively they are not really identical, and this can be demonstrated by asking pupils to rewrite the sentences so as to bring out the underlying meanings.

We cannot eat the hot food (weather/cat?) – 'food' is seen to be the object of 'eat'.

The hot cat (food/weather?) cannot eat – 'cat' is seen to be the subject of 'eat'.

We cannot eat in the hot weather (food/cat?) – 'weather' has a causal relationship to 'eat'.

Sometimes, potential ambiguities are resolved by surface features. For instance, the oft-cited confusion in 'I can smell cooking apples' is not a genuine ambiguity between 'I can smell (someone) cooking apples' and 'I can smell cooking apples (not eating apples)'. In speech the distinction is marked by differences in intonation and juncture, and in writing it *should* be marked by a hyphen. Nevertheless, there is potential ambiguity in sentences like 'The soldiers opened fire on the revolting tribesmen'.

One effective and quite entertaining way to explore underlying structures is through ambiguous headlines. Here, because of the omission of grammatical markers and punctuation, misconstructions can easily arise, as in old chestnuts like:

General flies back to front.
Fish talks at Grimsby.
Tied dog leads to gun.
Giant waves down tunnel.
Health service ban stays.

As well as interpreting the different meanings and discussing the grammatical rewriting needed to clarify them, pupils can be invited to invent their own, or bring in misleading headlines which they come across, for instance, the genuinely ambiguous 'British wounded on the way home'.

A transformational approach was also implied in the lesson on question formation (pp. 140–1). The suggestion was made there that questions are derived by transformations on statements, so that statements, are a 'kernel' sentence pattern in deep structure. Similarly pupils can explore other transformations (commands, passive voice, negative, etc.) and see if they can formulate explicit rules for them. Expansion games (p. 144) may be seen, too, as a way of generating sentences, and the notion developed that an infinite number of sentences can be generated by a limited set of grammatical rules. And the sentences themselves may be infinite if they are of the recursive type ('This is the house that Jack built...').

Perhaps one of the best ways of approaching the creative nature of grammar is through a discussion of language learning in early childhood. How is it that in just five years, without yet the conceptual ability to 'learn' grammar from instruction, and exposed to very inadequate samples of language (as studies of parents talking to their babies have shown), children nevertheless achieve such a practical mastery of grammar that they can generate completely new sentences, which may never have been uttered before? This is the mystery of language acquisition. Pupils can be asked to bring in tape recordings of younger brothers and sisters (it is possible that fond parents may even have kept recordings of your pupils when they were infants) and the stages in the development of children's grammar discussed. At first, babies' grammar is quite unlike adult grammar, but is yet recognizably structured. (What does this imply?) The playfulness of babies' language behaviour might be noted, and the delight in practising new structures. Particularly interesting are the 'good errors' made by children – 'mouses', 'I bringed it' – after they have already, at an earlier stage, said 'mice', and 'I brought it'. (What does this imply?)

Finally, it is important to stress the advice given earlier: the formal teaching of grammar can be successfully undertaken only by teachers who have themselves some grammatical knowledge and who feel confident in handling the kind of inductive enquiry advocated here. As the next chapter illustrates, there are many other kinds of objective language study which are accessible to a wider range of pupils and are of more immediate relevance and interest to them.

8
LANGUAGE STUDY
IN SCHOOLS

A study of language learning in early childhood, as suggested at the end of the preceding chapter, is fascinating in itself, regardless of any insight it might provide into the nature of grammar. In earlier chapters a number of language activities have been indicated which have a wider interest than the immediate concerns of spelling, punctuation or grammar. This chapter is concerned with the objective study of language in the secondary school: the aim is not to teach the pupils linguistics but for the teacher to use his own knowledge of linguistics to guide the pupils' curiosity about and interest in the language around them. Educating children to listen, talk, read and write also implies helping them to examine critically the nature of language and the ways in which it is used and misused. Many opportunities arise incidentally during the course of English lessons to comment on particular aspects of the pupils' own language, or language which they come across. Additionally, teachers may wish to adopt a more systematic, planned approach to language study using, perhaps, one of the course books or teachers' books which are now available (see Appendix I).

Language varieties

Children are naturally interested in the varieties of language found around them in their everyday life, and from the first form onwards can be encouraged to examine language varieties and raise questions concerning their appropriateness and the contexts of their use.

SECOND-YEAR, MIXED ABILITY

A discussion on accent, leading to a wider study of dialect, arises incidentally out of a reading of Walter de la Mare's poem 'The Listeners'. The school is situated in a North Midlands mining area, and the teacher notices that, when children read the poem, the vowel sounds in *stir* and *stair* are indistinguishable. She draws the children's attention to this, and they listen to each other reading the line, noting the different accents. (As well as the teacher, there are recent arrivals from South Wales and Birmingham, and several children who spent their early life in Scotland.) There follows a general discussion on how you can tell what part of the country someone comes from by his accent – television personalities are mentioned and also the accents of other teachers in the school. One boy recalls how the teacher's own 'posh' accent had caused difficulty when she first taught the class. The teacher asks whether they always speak with the same accent – she can understand them in school but often has difficulty understanding conversations overheard on the local bus – and the children agree that their accent is probably 'broader' at home or when talking to other children than it is in the classroom. The teacher introduces the word 'dialect', and explains it is not just a matter of accent – there are some words she had never heard until she moved north, for instance 'nesh' and 'mardy', while in her part of the world they 'brew' a cup of tea rather than 'mash' it. At this point she closes the discussion to return, somewhat belatedly, to the poem, but she asks them to quiz parents and grandparents at home and make a collection of dialect words. In a later lesson the class work in groups to produce dialect 'dictionaries', and a wall-chart is prepared headed 'How to understand a native of ―――――'.

THIRD-YEAR, TOP BAND (DOUBLE PERIOD)

The teacher plans to start the pupils thinking about some of the social connotations of accent. He has pre-recorded a short passage read in seven different accents: an extreme 'upper-class' accent, received pronunciation (southern), an 'educated' local accent, a broad local accent, Glaswegian, Geordie, and West Country. The pupils are told to listen carefully to the recordings and to see if they can guess anything about the speakers – where they come from, what sort of job they have, what sort of house they live in, what kind of people they are, and so on. After each person has spoken, the teacher stops the tape to allow the pupils to make a few notes. The class then divide into groups of five or six to share their opinions and to see if they can reach agreement about the voices. After about twenty minutes, the teacher asks the group 'secretaries' to report to the whole class and an interesting discussion ensues. It is suggested by one group that the Glaswegian is probably a criminal, by another a drunken football fan! The West Country man sounds 'jolly' and 'easy-going' – perhaps he is a farmer or, as one group says, 'a bit thick'. Particularly interesting is the hostility aroused in several groups by the upper-class accent – he would look down on you, you couldn't trust him, if he were a woman he would sound like Mrs Thatcher. There are corresponding speculations about the kind of jobs the speakers hold and the homes they live in. One group, however, wonders if you can really tell much about people from their accents other than where they live and, perhaps, in the case of the 'posh' accents, how they have been brought up. The teacher now tells the class that five of the seven recordings were made by one of his friends who was a skilled mimic, and raises with them the issue of stereotyping and prejudice associated with the way people speak. This prompts a wide-ranging discussion. The pupils generally feel they can vary their accents to some extent, and might do so, for instance, at an interview. One girl reports how her sister went to university and spoke with a different accent on her return. (Most noticeable had been the long ā sounds in 'pass', 'path', etc.) There is some discussion of why people feel some accents are preferable to others and whether this is justified or fair. At the end of the lesson the teacher sums up the main points which have emerged and asks the class, over the next week, to make a note of at least six different accents which they hear used on television or radio programmes, record who the speaker is, what is the topic, and what they think about the use of that accent in the programme.

FIRST-YEAR, MIXED ABILITY

The teacher brings in a book of children's playground games and chants recorded in a Nottingham primary school, and reads a few to the class. Many of the children recall similar games which they used to play, and the teacher explains how these games have been going on for many years, even centuries, quoting examples from the Opies' book. He asks how these games are passed on, and then whether the children have any 'secret' or 'private' forms of language among themselves. What does it mean, for instance, when someone is described as 'skill'? They tell him, and produce other examples of 'in' words (and one or two rather unsavoury 'in' jokes). He then asks them if they know any other kinds of 'slang' which people use to make them feel they 'belong' to a particular group. They discuss cockney rhyming slang, Citizens' Band slang, and air-force slang from the last war. He asks them to write a conversation between two people using slang in such a way as to make it difficult for an outsider to understand them: two school pupils, two football supporters, or two disco or pop fans.

FIFTH-YEAR, 'O' LEVEL LANGUAGE SET

The teacher has selected three sentences from essays recently written by the pupils: 'A poor family under these circumstances might well be affected personality-wise'; 'His death was due to the fact that he had been out in the bad weather all night'; 'The disadvantaged inhabit living conditions of low quality'. She has also written on the board a satirical leader from a national newspaper written in the style of Alexander Haig and full of American 'officialese'. Taking suggestions from the pupils she composes on the board simpler and more straightforward versions of what was intended. (Is the second sentence equivalent to 'He died from exposure'; does the third sentence mean more than 'Poor people live in poor housing'?) She then raises the general question of jargon and circumlocution. Why might people want to wrap up and disguise their meaning in 'cotton-wool' language? She provides three examples to focus their discussion: in the House of Commons, members are not allowed to call each other liars – what might they say instead; why do old-fashioned business letters use convoluted phraseology; why do we speak of someone having 'passed away' or 'gone to his rest' or even 'kicked the bucket'? After some discussion they reach the conclusion that at times jargon and circumlocution may be justified, but at other times (as in the newspaper article) it serves only to obscure the meaning and mystify the reader. Finally she asks the pupils *either* to imagine they have been accused of an offence, and write a letter to the court disguising the facts (without actually telling lies) and spinning the incident out so as to obscure the truth *or* to write a critique of a play or musical event saying, in effect, 'It was rubbish', but doing so in veiled and politely-phrased terms. For once, she says, she will be awarding marks for how *badly* they write!

Language functions

Children, and adults too for that matter, when asked what language is used for, tend to seize upon its communicative function – 'to tell other people something', 'to let other people know what you're thinking', 'to express your ideas'. Although this is, perhaps, the most prominent use in educational institutions, it is only one function among many. Children can be encouraged to examine the rich diversity of everyday language uses, both written and, especially, spoken.

FOURTH-YEAR, CSE GROUP

The class are used to role-playing and working out unscripted dramas. As part of a theme on personal relationships, the pupils are working in threes – mother, father, and son or daughter – having an argument about the offspring coming in late at night. The teacher asks them to prepare two short scenes, one in which the argument develops into a furious row, and the other in which an agreed compromise results. She then selects groups to act one or other of the scenes in front of the class, who are instructed to watch out for features of the behaviour and language of the participants which led to the different outcomes. Among other things to emerge from the discussion are a realization that *the way* in which something is said is often more important than *what* is said, and an awareness that language can be used to influence the behaviour and feelings of others. For homework, the teacher asks the class to write two contrasting dialogues between a policeman and a teenager whom he had stopped to question, one ending amicably, the other in confrontation.

A useful exercise with older pupils is to get them to think through an imaginary day, listing all the situations in which they use, or are subjected to, language – getting up, breakfast, walking to school, assembly, lessons, break, etc. They can be asked to think about what language is used for in each of these situations, and to keep a record of the kinds and purposes of language used during a typical day. The teacher will need to provide a framework of the main language functions for pupils to work from.

SECOND-YEAR, MIXED ABILITY

Each child brings into the lesson a newspaper or magazine, and working in groups of about six they search for different kinds of writing for different purposes – news stories, gossip articles, sports pages, fashion pages, advertisements, horoscopes, feature articles, advice columns, and so on. The teacher then collects from the groups examples of different kinds of writing and discusses with the class the reasons for the differences. Each group has to cut out and mount a wall display, 'Read all about it', illustrating as many different kinds of writing as they can find. (Later on in the term the groups prepare and produce their own magazines.)

One of the major and perhaps most insidious functions of language is to persuade. The English teacher should help pupils to be aware of and on their guard against the more meretricious aspects of the language of persuasion.

THIRD-YEAR, MIXED ABILITY

The teacher circulates among the pupils several advertisements which he has cut from current periodicals, and writes on the board an American advertisement:

> If you want love interest to thrive, then try this dainty way – For this way is glamorous! It's feminine! It's alluring – Instinctively, you prefer this costly perfume of Arcadia Soap – It's a fragrance men love. Massage each tiny ripple of your body daily with this delicate, cleansing lather – Thrill as your senses are kissed by Arcadia's exquisite perfume. Be radiant.

The teacher poses to the class this question: 'The advertiser wants you to part with your money to buy his product. How does he persuade you to do this?' He has chosen the advertisements so that he can guide the discussion along three mains lines:

(*i*) attracting the readers' attention – brand names, slogans, colour, attractive/humorous pictures, etc.;

(*ii*) appealing to the readers' needs – a woman at the centre of an admiring circle of men, fear of social ostracism, the use of young couples, babies, luxurious cars, etc.;

(*iii*) the persuasive language of advertisements. Here the teacher asks the class to try to separate verifiable facts from opinions. The American advertisement, for instance, produces one verifiable fact, 'This soap is expensive.' The question is then raised: if the language in the advertisement is not generally used for imparting information, what is it used for? The class suggest that it makes the products 'sound' wonderful and makes you want to buy them. The words 'dainty', 'glamorous' and 'alluring' are picked out. One girl notices that 'each tiny ripple of your body' amounts to a subtle flattery, as does 'instinctively, you prefer – '. Another girl suggests one could translate 'massage each tiny ripple' into 'rub each small wrinkle' with consequent deflation of the effect. This seems a promising technique, so the class continue to debunk the advertisement: 'fragrance' becomes 'smell', and the pseudo-scientific grandeur of 'cleverly precision-blended in balanced perfection' becomes 'it was mixed carefully'. (For the follow-up lesson to this, see p. 112 Chapter 6.)

SECOND-YEAR, TOP BAND

The teacher has written on the board the following sets of headlines:

Super Spurs thrash feeble Forest.
Tottenham Hotspur 2 – Nottingham Forest 1.
Reds plucky fight in vain.

Strikers reject generous pay offer.
Union votes against accepting new wage rates.
Workers stand firm for fair deal on pay.

She asks the class if the headlines are 'neutral', of if they are biased towards one side or the other. The children pick out the words which indicate the bias: 'thrash', 'plucky', 'strikers reject' *v.* 'workers stand firm', and so on. She then presents a choice of neutral headlines: 'The American group, Joan Jett and the Blackhearts, opened their British tour last night', and 'Yesterday, the Argentine army retreated' and asks the class to write two contrasting reports, with appropriate headlines, as the news might be reported in a British and an Argentinian paper, or in a music magazine and a magazine which disapproved of 'pop'.

The meaning of meaning

A study of bias in language reminds us that most words do not have just a referential meaning, or one single, simple denotation. As R. G. Collingwood puts it:

> The proper meaning of a word ... is never something upon which the word sits perched like a gull on a stone; it is something over which the word hovers like a gull over a ship's stern.

The study of meaning is a fascinating topic and opportunities to explore 'the meaning of meaning' can occur in all areas of the English curriculum. Indeed, it might be argued that *meaning* lies implicitly at the heart of all English teaching; the problem is when to make it explicit.

FIRST-YEAR, MIXED ABILITY

The class are acting A. A. Milne's short play *The Ugly Duckling*. With fifteen minutes to spare at the end of the lesson the teacher asks them to look back at the 'ginger hippopotamus' exchange. (In this, the rather stupid suitor for the princess's hand is asked the riddle: 'What is it that purrs and likes milk?', to which he replies 'a hippopotamus'. Fortunately his quick-witted manservant explains that in one of the distant lands visited by his Highness, the natives gave the name 'hippopotamus' to a small, ginger furry animal which purred when you stroked it.) She raises with them the conventional nature of meaning. Does it matter if we call a cat a hippopotamus? Is there anything particularly 'catty' about the name 'cat'? What about different languages – is 'dog' a more suitable name than 'chien'? Do we ever invent names or change the meanings of words? (Where does 'yomping' come from? What about 'television'?) Some words, however, do seem to suggest their meanings by sounding like what they represent – cuckoo, clang, tinkle, perhaps yomping itself. She asks them if they know the collective nouns for sheep, cows, lions, geese – they agree that perhaps 'gaggle of geese' and 'pride of lions' do seem particularly appropriate. For homework she asks the class to make up five collective nouns of their own (for teachers, school children – she thinks a 'chatter of children', but perhaps they can do better – milkmen, disc-jockeys, and one other), and five onomatopoeic words (for an alarm-clock, an electric drill, a butterfly, electricity pylons, and one other).

THIRD-YEAR, MIXED ABILITY

The lesson starts with some quick practice on looking up the meaning of words in personal dictionaries. The teacher then raises the questions: 'How do *dictionaries* arrive at their definitions? How do we know we can trust them? If you didn't know the meaning of a word, and there were no dictionaries or experts to consult, how might you go about discovering the meaning?' The children consider one or two examples – dinghy, truthful, catastrophe – and soon realize that the meaning of a word depends on its use, and the physical and verbal contexts in which it occurs. The teacher suggests that one way to define the meaning of a word would be to give a number of typical contexts. She asks them to define the imaginary word 'slanky' from the following sentences, written on the board:

a. Some people feel slanky when they first get up in the morning.
b. Everyone feels slanky on a hot afternoon.
c. If you want to get over that slanky feeling, take Zippo vitamin pills.
d. I'm not cross, just slanky.
e. The slanky, slanky bluebell,
    That droops upon its stem.
    (Adapted from S. I. Hayakawa, *Language in Thought and Action*.)

She explains that this is how big dictionaries do illustrate meanings, and reads the entries for 'dinghy', 'truthful' and 'catastrophe', from the *OED*. She describes how dictionaries are compiled and how they are continually being brought up to date as the language changes. Finally she asks them each to compile three entries for a '_____ School Dictionary' for such terms as 'English lesson', 'school dinner', 'assembly' — with suitable illustrative sentences!

In a later lesson, the same class continue to explore word-meanings, looking at words with multiple meanings, and words with related meanings. The teacher starts by asking for a definition of 'head', and then queries how its use in 'The head caned all the boys' fits this definition. The pupils volunteer other meanings (head of a spear, head of a mountain, head start, matters came to a head, etc.), and the teacher uses the blackboard to suggest that a word has an *area* of meaning, rather than one precise meaning. She indicates the central or core meaning of head, with other usages more or less closely related to this central meaning. She asks the pupils to write sentences containing as many different senses of the words 'pool' and 'strike' as they can think of. She collects together their ideas and discusses, using the blackboard, the areas of meaning of these two words. Finally, she moves on to synonyms, and asks for the meaning of 'steed'. 'Horse' is suggested, and she asks what is wrong with the sentence, 'The rag-and-bone man's steed pulled his old cart through the dirty back streets of the town.' Again, she uses a blackboard diagram to demonstrate that two words, such as horse and steed, are hardly ever exact synonyms – that, while there is some area of overlap, there are many contexts in which 'horse' can be used but not 'steed', and perhaps a few contexts in which 'steed' is used but 'horse' would be inappropriate. As a final exercise the class try to map on to the blackboard diagram words like 'nag', 'charger', 'mount' and 'gee-gee'.

SECOND-YEAR, TOP BAND

While reading *King Richard's Land* the class come across a passage in which 'the pale resolute face' of Archbishop Sudbury is contrasted to the face of Wat Tyler 'red and swollen with triumph'. The crowd is said to 'roar like a savage beast' and to 'give a throaty yell of triumph'. The teacher asks whom the author wants us to sympathize with, and how we can tell that. Towards the end of the lesson she returns to discuss the passage, and points out that many words have an emotional tone to them as well as a 'factual' meaning – as well as conveying information about an object they persuade us to take an attitude towards that object. For instance, she says, while I am slim and slender, you are just thin, and she is positively scrawny and scraggy. She writes the 'declension' on the board, and with the class works on the declension of 'I say what I mean' ('You are blunt/outspoken', 'He is rude/always putting his foot in it'). She asks the class to work on the declensions of 'You are fat', 'I am firm and determined', 'You gossip'. A lively discussion ensues when they pool their ideas.

For homework she asks them to write the opening paragraph of two stories describing the appearance of the same central character; in one of the stories he is to be the hero, in the other the villain.

Language and society

Many of the social aspects of language have already been touched upon in earlier chapters, especially attitudes towards language and the notions of 'correct' and 'incorrect' usage. Opportunities for making explicit the social context of language use will often arise in school. For instance, a teacher may judge from a class's reaction to words like 'gay' or 'queer' that it would be appropriate to discuss how social change can cause linguistic change. There are numerous examples from earlier periods of similar linguistic change, and it could make an interesting topic to explore how and why words change their meanings. This could open up, at a more sophisticated level, the issue of whether words have a 'proper' meaning, and whether it matters if words change their meaning. (Is the loss of certainly 'gay' and perhaps 'queer' to be deplored?)

FOURTH-YEAR, CSE GROUP, SOCIAL STUDIES

Arising out of work on the role and place of women in society, the teacher raises the question of sexism in language. Why, for instance, does it always have to be the *chairman* of a meeting or the *spokesman* for a cause? Why, about mixed company, is it correct to say 'Everyone has *his* own opinion'? She claims that even school books use this kind of language, and quotes examples from the EOC booklet *Ending Sex-Stereotyping in Schools*:

> Man invented the wheel.
> The pioneers moved West, taking their wives and children with them.

She asks the class whether they think this kind of sexism in language matters, and what can be done about it. A lively discussion ensues under her skilful questioning. One would only comment that some linguistic knowledge about the widespread use of 'marked/unmarked' pairs of words and structures throughout languages might have helped her (and her pupils) to distinguish the social arguments from the linguistic ones.

Language also indicates status and power relationships in society. Not only what is said but the way in which it is said can tell us much about the roles people play and the relationships between them. For instance, Thames Television's booklet *Language* has the following ingenious comparison between the language of employer and worker.

Employer	*Worker*
I am an employer.	He's the boss.
She is an employee.	I'm a worker.
She is a packaging operative grade II.	I put things in boxes.
She is semi-skilled.	I'm bored stiff.
Each day she lunches in our on-site cafeteria.	Every day I have my dinner in the works canteen.
But we are currently rationalizing our manpower requirements.	They're giving us the sack.
She will then be entitled to unemployment benefits.	I can get the dole.
Pending such time as she secures further employment.	Till I get another job, if I get another job.

The resulting exercise asks pupils to write their own language exchanges between, say, a doctor and a patient beginning: 'I am a medical consultant' – 'He's my GP.' (*Language*, Thames Television/Hutchinson, p. 24.)

The phonology of English

The phonology of English provides an excellent introduction to the notion of linguistic structure.

SIXTH-FORM, GENERAL STUDIES

The teacher begins by posing the question of which sounds the pupils had difficulty pronouncing in French and German. Why was this? Do foreigners have the same sort of difficulty pronouncing English? He then asks them to write down all the different sounds which we use in English. These are sorted on the board into consonants and vowels. The problem of representing sounds soon emerges – *sh* stands for one sound, *th* stands for one of two distinct sounds (this, thin), while *x* does not represent any separate sound – vowels have to be listed using illustrative words, f*air*, *owl*, etc. The teacher gives one or two examples of how phoneticians overcome this difficulty by using a phonetic alphabet. He then starts the group thinking about how sounds are produced – which vocal organs are used in producing particular sounds, and what is the basic difference between consonants and vowels. He focuses attention on the place of the tongue in the mouth and the position and shape of the lips. By asking questions on the similarities and differences among consonants he develops the idea of contrasting pairs, e.g.

b/p   b/m
d/t   d/n
g/k   g/ng

By examining closely the production of vowel sounds, the pupils are led to realize that most English long vowels are, in fact, diphthongs. And this leads back to the difficulty of foreign language pronunciation – we have problems because the sounds of a foreign language are similar to but not identical with the sounds we use in English. The lesson concludes with the class trying out some non-English phonemes: the pure vowels of French, the Welsh -ll-, and the Scots -ch sound in 'loch'.

A second lesson begins with the teacher reminding the group of the work done previously and they briefly recapitulate the phonemic structure of English. He then asks them if they can hear any difference between the *t* sounds in *tile* and *stile*. They test the difference by holding the backs of their hands close to their mouths, when the puff of air in *tile* can be felt, and by whispering the words when the aspirated *t* can be clearly heard. The teacher then asks about the c sound in *keel* and *cool*, and the group feel the different positions of the tongue moving back through keel, kill, curl, call, cool. The teacher points out that these are, clearly, different sounds, and some languages might well distinguish between them – a 'k^{i}ol' with a front k might be a different object from a 'k^{u}ol' with a back k, and it might make all the difference in the world whether you called your girl-friend a 't^{h}ol' or a 'tol'. Why do we not recognize the difference in English? With prompting from the teacher, the class realize that the differences are not significant in English because they are not genuine alternatives, but are fully determined by their context. What we hear as one sound is really an amalgam of many related sounds whose differences are not significant for us. As babies, the teacher explains, we learn the sound-structure of our mother-tongue so thoroughly that, in later life, we have difficulty hearing, let alone producing, sounds which are not significant in our language. The same is true of combinations of sounds. The class have difficulty pronouncing 'ngthestr' – it is clearly a non-English word – even though 'strength' presents no problems. Finally the teacher describes the problems he had once trying to learn a West African language, and the pupils have fun practising esoteric sounds – trills, clicks, implosives, and so on.

FIRST-YEAR, MIXED ABILITY, INTEGRATED STUDIES

The children have been following a half-term theme on ancient civilizations, during which they have found out about ancient scripts and traced the development of the modern alphabet. The teacher asks them why English is a difficult language to spell, and collects from them examples of how the same spelling (-ough) can represent different sounds and the same sound can be represented in different ways (hair, there, care, pear, etc.). He then suggests how much easier it might be if there were just one symbol for every sound, and he sets them the task of devising their own English alphabet. They should (*i*) try to work out how many different sounds there are in English and (*ii*) invent an alphabet, drawing if they wish upon their knowledge of ancient scripts. Some of the children need a lot of help with the first part of the task and towards the end of the lesson the teacher finds it necessary to discuss with the class the sounds for which they will need symbols.

In a later lesson he shows them an example of a modern attempt at a semi-phonemic script (i.t.a.), discusses with them some of the problems of spelling reform, and asks them to find out about modern scripts which do not use the Roman alphabet.

History of the language

Some aspects of the historical study of English, namely the development of spelling, punctuation and grammar, have already been discussed in previous chapters, but the English language is a rich mine for all kinds of historically-based work, much of it appropriate for interdisciplinary humanities courses. English is the language of an island race, forged over the centuries from the contact of native speakers with wave upon wave of invaders and, more recently, from colonial expansion. A study of loan-words, for instance, is itself a study of the panorama of English history. To take a specific example, after a first-year class have studied the Anglo-Saxon and Viking invasions, their English teacher might want to look at loan-words from that period. He might give examples of Celtic words which remain in English and ask what sort of words they are, and why so few have survived. He might look at the geographical distribution of Danish and Anglo-Saxon place names, and discuss the existence of pairs like kirk/church. He could ask what kinds of words the Anglo-Saxons would be likely to borrow from the Vikings, and give examples of them. Similar study can be undertaken in connection with the conversion of Britain and spread of Christianity, the Norman Conquest and the Middle Ages, the revival of learning and the Renaissance, the age of discovery and colonization, the wars of the nineteenth and twentieth centuries, the rise to a world power of America – all these have left their mark on the language we speak today. An entertaining exercise is to draw up a list of loan-words, get pupils to guess their origins, then hunt them up in a dictionary. A typical list of ten words might be: crag, gin, legal, potato, reindeer, school, thermometer, toboggan, violin, wardrobe.

A sense of the ways in which the language has changed may be gained by looking at written extracts from different periods or, if the teacher is willing to attempt it, by reading passages from, say, *Beowulf*, *Sir Gawain*, Chaucer and Shakespeare in their contemporary pronunciation. The most important outcome of this kind of study is the realization that our language is a living language which is still changing today. A glance at the supplements to the *OED* illustrates how words are continually entering the language, acquiring new meanings, or dropping out. How many pupils, for instance, understand now what 'flower-power' means? How long will 'skate-board' last? However did we manage without 'television'? Am I old-fashioned if I talk about a 'wireless'? Does it matter if children write 'It was a nice day' – more importantly, shall I be understood if I refer to 'a nice point'?

Pronunciation changes too, albeit more slowly. Listen to the vowel sound in 'off' as spoken by an old person, or on an old recording. Some words change in the direction of their spelling ('forehead', 'towards', 'waistcoat' – I have heard a teacher pronounce the -c- in 'victuals'). Transatlantic influences have created alternative pronunciations and uncertainty, especially about stress – does it matter if we say 'advértisement' or 'advertísement', 'hárass' or 'haráss', 'kílometre' or 'kilómetre'?

A study of the history of the language helps children to regard their mother tongue not as a fossilized skeleton fixed for ever in some kind of 'ideal' form, but as a living, changing corpus with which they can be inventive and creative.

Language and languages

Finally, there are many questions about the nature of language itself which provide interesting topics for discussion. How did language start? What do we know of so-called 'primitive' languages? How plausible is the account of the origins of language given in, say, *The Inheritors* or *Quest for Fire*? If you had to invent an early language, what would it look like?

Which language(s) is English most closely related to? How do we know? What happens to English if we trace it back in history? What are some of the other major language families and how do they differ from Indo-European? Roughly how many languages are there in the world, and how many of these are literate? Does it matter if a language dies out?

Does language really differentiate man from other species? Do animals have language, and what are the differences between animal and human language? What success has been achieved in teaching apes to use language?

Are there other 'languages' besides spoken and written language (for instance, sign language, chess notation, 'the language of mathematics')? Do we communicate only through language? The study of non-verbal communication, especially body-language, might provide an appropriate topic for a wet Friday afternoon!

Language is part of the warp and woof of our everyday lives. From morn till night we are immersed in language. The aim of this chapter has been to indicate ways in which the English teacher can help pupils to examine objectively their mother tongue and to develop a critical awareness of its uses and misuses. The alert teacher will continually be on the look-out for examples which are fresh and topical, and arise in the pupils' own experience. Above all, he will seek to make pupils sensitive to the use of language in their everyday lives, so that they become the masters of language and not its victims.

PART THREE
REFERENCE SECTION

APPENDIX I
ANNOTATED BIBLIOGRAPHY

A. General

Bullock Report: *A Language for Life* (London, HMSO, 1975).

Dunsbee, T. and Ford, T., *Mark My Words* (London, Ward Lock, 1980). A study of the ways in which teachers mark work and the effect this has on pupils.

Gatherer, W. A., *A Study of English* (London, Heinemann, 1980).

Smith, F., *Writing and Writers* (London, Heinemann, 1982). Both have interesting sections on spelling, punctuation and grammar.

Shaughnessy, M. P., *Errors and Expectations* (New York, Oxford University Press, 1977). Subtitled 'A guide to the teacher of basic writing', this is full of useful ideas and examples, albeit based on the writing of American college students; includes sections on spelling, punctuation, syntax and common errors.

Thornton, G., *Teaching Writing* (London, Arnold, 1980).

B. Course-books

It is expected that English teachers will choose course-books for the contributions they make to the whole English curriculum. The treatment of spelling, punctuation and grammar is a relatively unimportant part of this, especially since much of this work should be done with individual pupils, as the need arises. No course-book, therefore, can be recommended on these grounds; on the other hand, many course-books provide exercises which the teacher may select from and use with pupils from time to time.

However, there has appeared on the market in recent years a different kind of course-book, providing a wider approach to the study of language (see Chapter 8). A selection of these books is given in B(ii).

(I) BASIC SKILLS

Brindley, D. J., *Excellence in English*, 5 vols (London, Hodder & Stoughton, 1978). Full of lively ideas for teaching spelling and punctuation, with a good summary of the uses of basic punctuation marks.

Beecroft, R. and Sanderson, G., *Perspectives in English*, 2 vols (London, Hart-Davis, 1982).

Seely, J., *Oxford Secondary English*, 3 vols and teachers' books (Oxford, Oxford University Press, 1982).

Sweeney, T. and Maguiness, R. J., *Challenge*, 3 vols (London, Hodder & Stoughton, 1972). All three of these series separate the specific language exercises from the main text, so that the teacher may dip into them at his discretion.

Thomson, O. M., *From Reading to Writing* (Oxford, Oxford University Press, 1979).

Proud, A., *Upgrade your English* (London, Arnold, 1980).

Thomson, O. M., *The Craft of Writing* (Oxford, Oxford University Press, 1980). These three are intended for GCE/CSE language work, the last two using proof-reading as a teaching technique.

(II) LANGUAGE STUDY

Eagleson, R. D. (ed.), *Wordswork* (Methuen of Australia, 1979). Stimulating language extracts for discussion and analysis from sport, news, humour, politics, etc.

Forsyth, I. and Wood, K., *Language and Communication*, 2 vols (London, Longman, 1977).

Foster, J. *et al.*, *Communicate* (London, Macmillan, 1981). A collection of practical tasks and exercises.

Goldenberg, S. *et al.*, *Language* (London, Thames TV/ Hutchinson, 1979). Material for discussion on language issues, based on a Schools TV series.

Healey, M., *Your Language*, 3 vols (London, Macmillan, 1981). A lively and wide-ranging course.

Newby, M., *Making Language*, 3 vols (Oxford, Oxford University Press, 1981).

C. Spelling

(I) GENERAL BACKGROUND

Diringer, D., *A History of the Alphabet* (London, Unwin, 1977).

Hornsby, B. and Shear, F., *Alpha to Omega* (London, Heinemann, 1980).

Jensen, H., *Sign, Symbol, Script* (London, Allen & Unwin, 1970).

Peters, M. L., *Spelling: Caught or Taught?* (London, Routledge & Kegan Paul, 1967).

Peters, M. L., *Success in Spelling* (Cambridge, Cambridge Institute of Education, 1970). An account of the research on which her earlier book is based.

Scragg, D. S., *A History of English Spelling* (Manchester, Manchester University Press, 1974).

Stubbs, M., *Language and Literacy* (London, Routledge & Kegan Paul, 1980). Especially Chapter 3, 'Some principles of English spelling'.

Venezky, R. L., *The Structure of English Orthography* (The Hague, Mouton, 1970).

(II) PRACTICAL MATTERS

Cotterell, G., *Diagnosis in the Classroom* (Centre for the Teaching of Reading, Reading, University of Reading, School of Education).

Garrett, M., *English Corrected* (London, Heinemann, 1980).

Moorhouse, C. (ed.), *BBC Writing and Spelling Handbook* (London, BBC Publications, 1979). Although primarily intended for adults with writing problems, full of practical suggestions which will be especially useful with older secondary-school pupils.

Peters, M. L., *Diagnostic and Remedial Spelling Manual* (London, Macmillan, 1975).

Peters, M. L. and Cripps, C., *Catchwords: Ideas for Teaching Spelling* (New York, Harcourt, Brace, Jovanovich, 2nd edn, 1980). The first 24 pages offer sound general guidance.

Pollock, J., *Signposts to Spelling* (London, Heinemann, 1980). Ideas to help the teacher help individual pupils.

Smith, A. B., *The Teaching of Spelling* (Bradford, Schools Psychological Service).

Torbe, M., *Teaching Spelling* (London, Ward Lock, 1978). Probably the single most useful book on spelling for the teacher; sound, practical advice.

Finally, there are a number of books intended to help adults with their spelling, which a teacher may find helpful in providing ideas for workcards, trouble-spots, spelling rules, etc.; one or more of these might be a useful work of reference:

Fergus, P. M., *Spelling Improvement* (New York, McGraw Hill, 3rd edn, 1978).

Metcalfe, J. E., *The Right Way to Spell* (Tadworth, Elliot Right Way Books, 1980).

Thornhill, P., *Spelling Made Easy* (London, Teach Yourself Books, 1976).
Wright, W. D., *Learn to Spell* (Welwyn, Nisbet, 1975).

(III) SPELLING DICTIONARIES

It is anticipated that all children will have ready access to an ordinary dictionary. One of the following might provide a useful supplementary work of reference in a classroom:

Fimberg, L. B. and D., *Cassell's New Spelling Dictionary* (London, Cassell, 1976).
Kirkpatrick, E. M. and Schwartz, C. M., *Spell Well* (London, Chambers, 1980).

D. Punctuation

Bailey, R. E., *A Survival Kit for Writing English* (London, Longman, 1977). Has a useful section on punctuation.
Williams, E., *Assignments in Punctuation and Spelling* (London, Arnold, 1977). Useful ideas and exercises for the teacher to choose from.

And a number of books which the teacher may find useful as reference books to consult on aspects of punctuation:

Carey, G. V., *Mind the Stop* (Harmondsworth, Penguin, 1971).
de Larrabeiti, M., *Full Marks* (London, Macmillan, 1981).
Gordon, I., *Practical Punctuation* (London, Heinemann, 1978).
Herd, H., *Everybody's Guide to Punctuation* (London, Allen & Unwin, 1975).
Smith, A. J., *Clear Punctuation* (Cambridge, University Tutorial Press, 1981).

E. Grammar

(I) GRAMMAR TEACHING

Currie, W. B., *New Directions in Teaching English Language* (London, Longman, 1973).

Fraser, H. and O'Donnell, W. R. (eds), *Applied Linguistics in the Teaching of English* (London, Longman, 1969).

Both these books compare traditional and modern approaches to grammar teaching.

Gilliland, J., *Readability* (London, University of London Press, 1972). Chapter 7 is called 'Beyond the sentence', and there is a discussion of paragraph structure on pp. 74–9.

Open University, Course PE 232: Language development, Block 2, *Patterns of language* (Milton Keynes, Open University Press, 1979). Contains some interesting practical exercises.

Quirk, R. and Smith, A. H. (eds), *The Teaching of English* (Oxford, Oxford University Press, 1964). Chapters 2 and 5 are about grammar teaching.

Wilkinson, A., *The Foundations of Language* (Oxford, Oxford University Press, 1971). Pp. 32–5 summarize the evidence on the effectiveness of grammar teaching.

(II) CORRECTNESS AND USAGE

Mittins, W. H., 'What is correctness?', reprinted in Wade, B. (ed.), *Language Perspectives* (London, Heinemann, 1982).

Mittins, W. H. *et al.*, *Attitudes to English Usage* (Oxford, Oxford University Press, 1970). A research account which might prove helpful to teachers who want pupils to undertake projects in this area.

Philp, A. W., *Attitudes to Correctness in English* (London, Longman, 1968).

The standard works on English usage, by Partridge and

Fowler, are both prescriptive and rather conservative in approach. More flexible are:

Fieldhouse, H., *Everyman's Good English Guide* (London, Dent, 1982).

Gowers, E., *The Complete Plain Words* (London, HMSO, 2nd edn, 1973).

Hudson, K., *The Dictionary of Diseased English* (London, Macmillan, 1977). The introduction is worth reading, too, for a spirited defence of 'standards' in English and an attack on 'bad' English.

Thompson, D., *The Nelson Guide to Good English* (London, Nelson, 1976).

F. Language study

(I) LINGUISTICS AND ENGLISH TEACHING

Gannon, P. and Czerniewska, P., *Using Linguistics: An Educational Focus* (London, Arnold, 1980).

Keen, J., *Teaching English: A Linguistic Approach* (London, Methuen, 1978).

Stork, F. C., 'Language study in secondary education', in *English in Education*, Vol. 14, No. 1, 1980, and the ensuing debate in this and subsequent issues.

(II) TEACHING MATERIALS – GENERAL

Doughty, A. *et al.*, *Language in Use* (London, Arnold, 1971). An invaluable source book.

Doughty, A. and P., *Using 'Language in Use'* (London, Arnold, 1974).

Raleigh, M. *et al.*, *The Languages Book* (London, ILEA English Centre, 1981).

See also the course books listed under B(II).

(III) LANGUAGE VARIETIES

Hughes, A. and Trudgill, P., *English Accents and Dialects* (London, Arnold, 1979).

O'Donnell, W. R. and Todd, L., *Variety in Contemporary English* (London, Allen & Unwin, 1980).

Opie, I. and P., *The Lore and Language of Schoolchildren* (St Albans, Paladin, 1977). A fascinating study of children's playground language.

Orton, H. and Wright, N., *A Word Geography of England* (London, Seminar Press, 1974).

Schur, N. W., *English English* (Connecticut, Verbatim Books, 2nd edn, 1980). A comparison of British and American English from an American point of view.

Wakelin, M. F., *English Dialects* (London, Athlone Press, 1972).

(IV) HISTORICAL ASPECTS

Aitchison, J., *Language Change: Progress or Decay?* (London, Fontana, 1981).

Barber, C., *Linguistic Change in Present-day English* (London, Oliver & Boyd, 1964).

Baugh, A. C., *A History of the English Language* (London, Routledge & Kegan Paul, 1951).

Davies, C. S. and Levitt, J., *What's in a Name?* (London, Routledge & Kegan Paul, 1970). On place names.

Foster, B., *The Changing English Language* (London, Macmillan, 1968).

Potter, S., *Changing English* (London, André Deutsch, 1969).

See also books on the history of spelling and alphabets listed under C(i), and the history of grammar and usage listed under E(ii).

(V) LANGUAGE USE AND MISUSE

Packard, V., *The Hidden Persuaders* (Harmondsworth, Penguin, 2nd edn, 1981). A classic exposé of the advertising industry and the main reference for this section.

Dyer, G., *Advertising as Communication* (London, Methuen, 1982). A horse of a very different colour from the media studies stable.

Hayakawa, S.I., *Language in Thought and Action* (London, Allen & Unwin, 1952).

Hayakawa, S.I., *The Use and Misuse of English* (New York, Fawcett, 1962).

'Vigilans', *Chamber of Horrors* (London, André Deutsch, 1952). British and American jargon exposed.

Appendix II (see p. 82)

Hints on pronunciation for foreigners
I take it you already know
Of tough and bough and cough and dough?
Others may stumble but not you,
On hiccough, thorough, laugh and through?
Well done! And now you wish, perhaps
To learn of less familiar traps?

Beware of heard, a dreadful word
That looks like beard and sounds like bird,
And dead: it's said like bed, not bead —
For goodness sake don't call it 'deed'!
Watch out for meat and great and threat
(They rhyme with suite and straight and debt).

A moth is not a moth in mother
Nor both in bother, broth in brother,
And here is not a match for there
Nor dear and fear for bear and pear,
And then there's does and rose and lose —
Just look them up — and goose and choose,
And cork and work and card and ward,
And font and front and word and sword,
And do and go and thwart and cart —
Come, come, I've hardly made a start!
A dreadful language? Man alive!
I'd mastered it when I was five!